Prayerbook
for a Domestic Priest

essential prayers
for husbands and fathers

by andrew schmiedicke

CHESTERTON PRESS

STRASBURG, VIRGINIA

Chesterton Press
Strasburg, Virginia

ISBN: 9798895902417

Printed in the United States of America

contents

Dedication:

To my children,
their spouses, and their children,
especially my sons, sons-in-law, and grandsons:
Faithfully pass on the one truth Faith
so that when Jesus Our Lord returns,
He will find faith upon the earth. (Luke 18:8)
Lex orandi, lex credendi.

foreword
by the author's wife

My husband and I are Catholics, and our religion requires a priest to lead the liturgy and administer the sacraments. Thus, our Church consists of clergy and laity. However, there is also the common priesthood of all the faithful who have been baptized into Christ Jesus, and the father of a family has a special role in being the domestic priest.

When I was a young college graduate, I worked for an apostolate called Catholics United for the Faith, which had been started by a convert, H. Lyman Stebbins, to respond to the call of the Second Vatican Council to mobilize the laity to discover their priesthood. He wrote a short red booklet called *The Priesthood of the Laity in the Domestic Church*, a book about home prayer life. I gave a copy to the man who would become my husband, and after we married, I dubbed him my domestic priest, a role he has filled admirably for the past thirty years.

Women tend to be more spiritual than men, so I have always seen a special genius in Christ's requirement that the man be the priest. It prods men to exercise that gift. And there is a fittingness, a complementariness about the man leading prayer for the family. I have no problem asking my husband to lead us in prayer, and he is comfortable doing so.

Not all men are, and some women are more inclined to lead prayers. But when women give space for the man to lead, a special charism is unleashed that graces the family.

Some families like to gather, light candles, and reflect. Some have a special prayer altar or place for prayer. We do too. But we also pray the rosary while driving in the car or taking a walk. Our family tends to dispense with quality time in favor of quantity time, utilizing the "It's got to happen NOW" model. Also, my husband figures there are more opportunities for the quality prayer time to happen if we have a quantity of appointed prayer times. We feel it's better to pray together even if it's a little hectic rather than waiting for the perfect moment. As the saying goes, "Practice makes perfect."

We move our prayer place according to the season: when spring days come, we pray our family Rosary outside, sometimes on a walk in the quiet of the evening. During cold fall and winter months, we huddle around the fireplace wood-burning stove to pray morning prayers.

The father as domestic priest is there to lead prayer, to model praying for his children, but specifically to intercede for his family, himself, his spouse, his children, and his ancestors—regardless of what everyone else's schedules or felt needs are. Fathers need to pray. Fathers *need* to lead their families in prayer, and it's wise for wives to recognize this and allow and encourage their husbands to lead prayers as they see fit.

The question of how much participation is required from children is a prudential one. We require both hyperactive toddlers and sulky teenagers to attend family prayer. But even if individual family members refuse or cannot be cajoled into participating, the parents should pray anyhow, because prayer is for our own benefit, not the Lord's. *We* need prayer. Without it, faith dies, hope is lost, and hearts grow cold to love. Building habits of prayer means that often prayer is messy and chaotic, and there are countless attempts to begin again to build the habit of prayer. But any good habit takes time, and prayer habits are worth the effort, over and over again.

It is also the role of the domestic priest to discern how much formal prayer his family can handle—and to figure out how to best motivate them to pray. My husband has used treats to woo the younger ones into prayer: "Ice cream for all those who pray the family rosary out loud!"

We allow children to sit, stand, or kneel during the rosary, as long as it is reasonably reverent, and we don't require absolute silence from small children during prayer. And he evaluates our family's prayer habits to see if he can motivate them to do more, to go further, to keep the soil tilled and the fallow ground broken up, so that our family is actively seeking the Lord. (Hosea 10:12) And my husband has leaned into the liturgical seasons of the Church to accomplish much of this: it's always helpful to introduce a new challenge in prayer during Lent or Advent.

The prayers contained here are a deliberate variety: you need not pray them all, and each domestic church should amend and personalize their plan of life according to their needs, available space, and circumstances.

Note that many Catholic prayers are meant to be prayed with responses: a leader begins the prayer, and those who hear the prayer respond. This is meant to be an echo of the prayers of the angels in heaven, who are portrayed as calling out to one another, "Holy, holy, holy is the Lord, God of Hosts!" (Isaiah 6:3) We've used "L" to indicate the part prayed by the father or leader and "R" to indicate the part that is prayed by the mother, children, or others.

Fathers have a difficult role: they are there to image to their children God the Father "from whom all fathers in heaven and earth take their name" (Ephesians 3:15). Obviously, every human father will fall short in some way.

But when they fail, they must point their children beyond themselves to the Father Who will never fail them.

It's in hope that this little book can show the way for fathers to take up the role of household priest that we offer this book of prayers, many of which my husband has used with our family throughout the years. May the Lord use it to bear much fruit!

Regina Doman
Shirefeld, Virginia

December 2025

introduction

"The family is, so to speak, the domestic church. In it, parents should, by their word and example, be the first preachers of the faith to their children." Lumen Gentium 11

Some Catholics might associate referring to married men as domestic priests as some newfangled thing that came about after the Second Vatican Council. However, seeing the father as a domestic priest is something that is attested to from the earliest days of the Church, and is even prefigured beforehand.

In the biblical book of Malachi, it is clear that God wants to turn the hearts of fathers to their children; and the hearts of children to their fathers, lest God come and strike the land with doom. (Malachi 4:6) God is speaking there of the family. The restoration and building up of the kingdom of God begins in the little kingdom of the family, the domestic church.

How is the family the domestic church?

> In the beginning…God created man in His own image, in the image of God He created him; male and female He created them. And God blessed them, and God said to them, "…<u>have dominion</u>…over every living thing that moves upon the earth"…The Lord God <u>took the man</u> and put him <u>in the garden</u> of Eden to till it and <u>keep it</u>. Genesis 1:1; 1:27-28; 2:15 [Emphases added]

With these passages from the Word of God, we can see that man is given a mission right from the very beginning of his creation to care and **_keep_** what is entrusted to him by God. When God is establishing His covenant with the Israelites, in Exodus 12:24 He charges fathers to "**_keep_**" what could be described as the "priestly religious duties" of the Passover ritual.

In the new covenant, St. Peter, the first pope, addresses Christians in his first letter, saying they are "…a chosen race, **a royal <u>priesthood</u>**, a holy nation, God's own people." And they are to declare the wonderful deeds of God Who called them "out of darkness into His marvelous light." (1 Peter 2:9)

In the last book of the Bible, Revelation 1:5b-6 speaks of Jesus Christ, "Who loves us and has freed us from our sins by His Blood and made us a kingdom, **<u>priests</u>** to His God and Father, to Him be glory and dominion for ever and ever. Amen."

In these scripture passages mentioned above, I see an allusion to the common priesthood shared by all those who are baptized into Christ Jesus, "the sole priest, in which all His members participate." (CCC 1141, quoting *Lumen Gentium* 10)

This is also attested to by the Church Fathers. St. Ambrose asks, "What is the people itself but priestly? ...Everyone is anointed to the priesthood." (On the Sacraments, 4, 1, 3)

St. Augustine asserts, "As we call all believers Christians on account of the mystical chrism, so we call all 'priests' because they are members of the one Priest." (*The City of God*, 20, 10)

St. Isidore also teaches that "the whole Church is consecrated by the unction of chrism, because each is a member of the eternal King and Priest." (*On the Offices of the Church*, 2, 26)

Because of this testimony, the *Catechism of the Catholic Church* can authoritatively teach that all those who are baptized into Christ Jesus, share in the common priesthood of Jesus Christ "the sole priest, in which all His members participate." (CCC 1141)

Now certainly, the ordained ministerial priesthood is distinct and of a much higher order and authority than this common priesthood of all the faithful. As noted in the *Catechism of the Council of Trent,*

It will readily be seen that what the Apostle Peter says of all the faithful: *You are a chosen generation, a kingly priesthood, a holy nation*, applies especially and with much greater reason to the ministers of the Church. (*Roman Catechism*, pg. 199-200)

Nevertheless, the same catechism also teaches that "all the faithful are said to be priests, once they have been washed in the saving waters of Baptism." Vatican II concurred saying that "the baptismal seal enables and commits Christians to serve God…and to exercise their baptismal priesthood by the witness of holy lives and practical charity." (CCC 1273/*Lumen Gentium* 10)

Lumen Gentium goes on and specifically says, "In what might be regarded as *the domestic Church*, the parents by word and example are the heralds of the faith with regard to their children." (par. 11. Emphasis added.) St. John Paul II elaborates on this in *Familiaris Consortio* saying,

By means of the sacrament of marriage…the Christian family is continuously vivified by the Lord Jesus…through the offering of one's life and through prayer. In this priestly role, the Christian family is called to be sanctified and to sanctify the ecclesial community and the world. (par. 55)

So the Church teaches that the family (father, mother, children) constitute a domestic church. In fact, in Article 7 on "The Sacrament of Matrimony" in the *Catechism of the*

Catholic Church, section VI is specifically titled "The Domestic Church":

And later on the same catechism states that…

> The Christian family is the first place of education in prayer. Based on the sacrament of marriage, the family is the "domestic church" where God's children learn to pray "as the Church" and to persevere in prayer. For young children in particular, daily family prayer is the first witness of the Church's living memory as awakened patiently by the Holy Spirit. (CCC par. 2685)

Positions, responsibilities, and rights in the Domestic Church

On January 4, 1954, Pope Pius XII addressed the Italian Catholic Union of Middle-School Teachers, saying in part, "families should not be allowed to believe that they have satisfied their duties toward their children when they have sent them off to school, giving no thought to working hand in hand with the teachers, on whom they *wrongly* think they can completely unload a part of their responsibilities."

In addition, Pope Pius XII in his encyclical on Christian education, says, quoting St. Thomas Aquinas, that "'…the **<u>Father is the principle</u>** of generation, of education and discipline and <u>of everything that bears upon the perfection of human life.</u>'" [Emphasis added.]

In his encyclical, "Near the Chair of Peter," on June 29, 1959, Pope John XXIII instructs, "**<u>Let the father of the family take the place of God</u>** among his children, and not only by his authority but by the upright example of his life…" [Emphasis added.]

So here we have two popes, two Vicars of Christ, telling fathers that *they* are God's vicars in their families, in the domestic Church!

Given that…

What are Fathers, as Domestic Priests, to do in the Domestic Church?

St. Augustine, over a thousand years ago, warned fathers:

> To every man then, if he is the head of his own house, ought the office of the Episcopate to belong, to take care how his household believe, that none of them fall into heresy, neither wife, nor son, nor daughter…bought at so great a price. (St. Augustine on Matthew 25:24ff; Sermon 44 XCIV. Ben.)

What a high office and responsibility husbands and fathers hold in the family!

Speaking to me and my friend, Viviano Rodriguez, after Sunday Mass at our parish one time, Father Michael Duesterhaus told us that he used to think that as a parish priest he had responsibility for all the souls in his parish.

But later he came to discover that a parish priest actually has responsibility for all the souls in the geographic jurisdiction of his parish!

Later I told my dad about this conversation. Regarding bishops, I gasped at how much more immense responsibility they must carry. I said I was glad to just be a husband and father who was only responsible for the souls of my wife and our ten children. Then my dad said, "…and their spouses, and their children." DAD!!!

But my dad is right. We husbands and fathers carry an ongoing responsibility. A husband and father has a priestly call in Christ Jesus to offer his life as a sacrifice to God for the immortal souls and eternal well-being of his wife and children…and to a certain extent their spouses and their children…a sacrifice that can have a generational impact. We must take the lead in family prayers; establish faith-based household rituals and customs; give correction, guidance, and blessings; and help our children love the Mass—for generations to come.

These tasks should not unduly fall on the mother. Neither should the wife nag her husband about it. Rather she can support him, encourage him, and lovingly communicate to him that he is needed for leading the liturgical life of their home, their little domestic church.

Lyman Stebbins, in *The Priesthood of the Laity in the Domestic Church* comments to parents:

We cannot effectively exercise our priesthood in the home, and the home cannot effectively be a little Church without a program, a cult, a Liturgy of the Family. (p. 16)

How vain it is to think about evangelization on a grand scale if we decline to work first on the tiny field of our own families! (p. 15-16)

Oh, let us hurry to tell our children the great news of our rescue by Jesus Christ crucified, Who paid for us the entire contents of His pierced Heart! Let us make haste in fear and love! (p. 20)

To that end, I have included in the appendix a ceremony for the formal installation of a father and mother as pastor and associate of the domestic church, taken from the same booklet. Is this ceremony necessary for the father and mother to be the pastor and associate of their domestic church? No. They are that by virtue of the sacraments of matrimony and baptism. Is this ceremony of value? Yes! It gives a formality and intentionality to those roles, to the mission of the domestic priest in the domestic church.

One thing that I am convinced of is that we need to be more intentional in living our Catholic faith as husbands, fathers, and priests of the domestic church. Perhaps there was a lack of intentionality and formality of Adam explicitly informing his wife, Eve, about God's command that then led to the Fall.

So I want to encourage husbands and fathers to be more intentional about living out the mission of being domestic priests in the domestic church because the building up of the kingdom of God begins as it began over two thousand years ago in a little home, in a little village, in a little land—in the little kingdom of the family; the Domestic Church.

Andrew Schmiedicke
Shirefeld, Virginia

December 2025

ECCE·AGNVS·DEI·QVI·TOLIT·PECCATA·MVNDI·

1

the father as a man of prayer

"He who humbles himself will be exalted, humility *is the foundation of prayer." CCC #2559. Luke 18:14*

What is prayer? Why pray? What is the point? What is the purpose of prayer? According to St. John Damascene, Doctor of the Church, and quoted in the CCC #2559, "Prayer is the raising of one's mind and heart to God."

Prayer is communication with God, and the ultimate end is communion with God—God Who is all life and love, "abounding in love and truth" (Psalm 86:15), "the Way, the Truth, and the Life." (John 14:6) As a father and domestic priest, a man is to manifest to his family the Fatherhood of God "from whence all fathers take their name." (Ephesians 3:15) Therefore, a domestic priest needs to cultivate a life of prayer – both speaking and listening to God – to be a son in union with God so he can manifest God to his family.

I've tried to keep a schedule of time for prayer throughout the day, as well as a weekly adoration hour one night a week. Our parish requires that men take the late night and early morning adoration hours for security and protection reasons. An exhortation by Father Vincent Bork spurred me to make it part of my plan of life.

Following the recommendations of those wiser than I, I have tried to cultivate a routine of prayer and sacrifice, faithfulness to my daily duties, and a tender devotion to Our Lady. This routine of prayer, penance and sacrifice paradoxically has led me to great freedom. A man desirous of protecting his wife and children from spiritual and moral harm had better be prepared and start by protecting himself from spiritual and moral danger…so he can better protect others, those who God has entrusted to his care.

Prayer is also an acknowledgement that we are not in control. As much as we fathers would want to be in control—or at least project that we are in control of everything—there are many things that are simply out of our control. So we need to be in communion with the One Who is absolutely in control of absolutely everything.

To this end, an indispensable tool is the examination of conscience at the end of each day before sleep. Personally, I pray the Act of Contrition (p. 76) and another prayer I've come to love, the prayer for daily neglects as well as the prayer for healing sleep, both on page 41. The habit of getting right with God is especially useful when anxiety or cares seem to conspire to destroy your peaceful sleep.

Still, sometimes a father may experience being awakened at night, whether to walk a crying baby, comfort a child, investigate some unusual sound, or some other reason. As difficult as that has been for me, so far, I've never had to get up in the middle of the night and flee to another country with my wife and baby like St. Joseph was told to do because of a murderous tyrant wanting to kill them. (Matthew 2:13) One epiphany I had was to realize that if I had trouble returning to sleep after such an interruption, I could use that time for prayer—either speaking to God in formal prayers or listening to Him by reading and meditating on His Word in sacred Scripture, or by reading other spiritual writings by the saints or other holy people.

This chapter contains prayers that have been personally useful to me in building a daily prayer routine. I don't pray all of them every day, but I have used them in different seasons as the scaffold to give a structure to my daily life.

A word on routine prayer: once rote prayers are memorized, it can be easy to race through them. Try to stay vigilant. Slow down. Think about what you are saying, and to Whom you are saying it.

The Seven Daily Praises

The Psalmist praises God seven times a day. (Psalm 119:164) The following praises are a combination of Old and New Testament Scriptures, compiled by Steve Bollman of the ministry Paradisus Dei as examples of prayers for fathers. Over the past decade, I have worked them into my life: they only take about less than a minute to pray, and before long I memorized them. I've included indications of when I pray them during my workday.

Upon rising from sleep:

O Lord God of Hosts, how lovely is Your dwelling place. One day within Your courts is better than a thousand elsewhere! I would rather be a doorkeeper in the house of the LORD than dwell in the tents of the wicked. Blessed are those who dwell in your house forever singing Your praises!

Morning prayer (prayed before beginning work):

O merciful Father, what is man that You should be mindful of him? Or mortal man that You should care for him? Yet to ransom a sinner, You gave away Your only beloved Son. How great is Your Name, O LORD our God, through all the earth!

Midmorning: (during a midmorning break)

O beloved Son of the Father, in Your light we see light. We behold the revelation of the Father, slow to anger, and abiding in compassion. O LORD, Your mercy is as high as the heavens and as deep as the netherworld. How great is Your Name, O LORD our God, through all the earth!

Noon: (before eating lunch)
O Spirit of Love, You transform us from glory unto glory into the image of the Only-Begotten of the Father. What You reveal to us now dimly as in a mirror You will one day reveal to us face to face. How great is Your Name, O LORD our God, through all the earth!

Midafternoon: (around three o'clock)
O Mystery of life and love! How sweet the path of those who find You abiding in their homes, who gaze upon the beauty of Your face and hear the sweet sound of Your voice. Praise to You, Lord of Heaven and Earth, for You have hidden these things from the wise and learned and revealed them to the pure of heart.

Evening: (before leaving work or eating supper)
O Emmanuel, how great Your love for those who serve You, how near Your presence to those who love You! You dwell with those gathered in Your Name. Stay with us, O LORD, for the day is far spent and evening presses. O Emmanuel, be ever near to us.

Night: (before going to sleep)
LORD, now You let Your servant go in peace according to Your word; for my eyes have seen the salvation which You have prepared for those who love You. How great is Your Name, O LORD our God, through all the earth!

Prayers of Daily Dedication

Offering yourself to God as the priest of your family and dedicating the day to Him gives a stable foundation to the days' activities. Here are several examples to pick from, personalize, or inspire you. As your children grow, encourage them to find one to make their own.

A Husband's Daily Prayer

1. As a husband I beseech Thee, O Triune God, make me unselfish, cheerful, trustful, thrifty, and a devoted companion. If/Since I am blessed by Fatherhood, I ask for the additional grace of helpfulness and good example. May our family be modeled upon the Holy Family. Amen.

2. Eternal Father, in union with the Immaculate Heart of Mary *(kiss your scapular)*, I offer You the Precious Blood of Jesus from all the altars throughout the world joining with it the offering of my every thought, word, and action of this day—purified by you, Blessed Mother, and you, St. Joseph, that it may be made worthy of Our Father in heaven.

3. Jesus, I desire today to gain every indulgence and merit I can, and I offer them together with myself to Mary Immaculate that she may best apply them to the interests of Thy Most Sacred Heart. O Precious Blood of Jesus, save us! Immaculate Heart of Mary, pray for us now and at the hour of our death! Most Sacred Heart of Jesus, have mercy on us!

4. Most Sacred Heart of Jesus, truly present in the Holy Eucharist, I consecrate my body and soul to be entirely one with Your Heart being sacrificed at every instance on all the altars throughout the world, giving praise to the Father, pleading for the coming of His Kingdom. Please receive this humble offering of myself and use me as You will for the glory of the Father and the salvation of souls. Most Holy Mother of God, never let me be separated from your Divine Son. Please defend and protect me as your special child. St. Joseph, pray for us. Thank you, Holy Family.

5. Jesus, You are my Savior. Please save me from the snares and traps of the enemy. Please help me to avoid evil and do good so that it is no longer I who live but You Who lives in me.

6. Thank You, Father, Son, and Holy Spirit, for the gift of a new day. I pray I may use it for the gaining of the Eternal Day in every way. Please help me to order this day and all my days aright that I may gain wisdom of heart. Amen.

7. O Jesus, through the Immaculate Heart of Mary, I offer you my prayers, works, joys, and sufferings of this day for all the intentions of your Sacred Heart in union with the Holy Sacrifice of the Mass throughout the world, for the salvation of souls, the reparation of sins, the reunion of all Christians, and in particular for the holy intentions of the Holy Father this month. Amen.

Daily renewal of Consecration to Mary

Jesus gave Himself totally and completely to the Blessed Virgin Mary. He Whom the universe cannot contain allowed Himself to be contained in the immaculate womb of His Mother Mary. If you have made a Total Consecration of yourself to Mary according to the method of St. Louis de Montfort, St. Maximilian Kolbe, or another method, here is a daily renewal of that consecration.

Immaculata, Queen and Mother of the Church, I renew my self-consecration to you for this day and for always so that you might use me for the coming of the kingdom of Jesus in the whole world. To this end I offer you all my prayers, actions, and sacrifices of this day.

Prayers to St. Joseph the Worker

Before beginning work:

St. Joseph, the Worker, Provider of the Holy Family, through your labor you provided for the needs of the Holy Family. Please help us to work well in union with God so that He may bless and prosper our work that it may bear fruit in eternal life.

Our Father… Hail Mary…

St. Joseph, the Worker, pray for us. Amen.

After finishing work:

St. Joseph, the Worker, thank you for helping us to work well in union with God. Through your intercession may God bless and prosper the work of our hands that it may bear fruit in eternal life.

Hail Mary… Glory be…
St. Joseph, the Worker, pray for us. Amen.

The following is a prayer attributed to Pope St. Pius X asking St. Joseph to obtain from God the grace to work well. I usually pray this when beginning my work in the office.

O Glorious St. Joseph, model of all those devoted to labor, obtain for me the grace to work in a spirit of penance for the expiation of my many sins; to work conscientiously, putting the call of duty above my natural inclinations; to work with thankfulness and joy, considering it an honor to employ and to develop by means of labor the gifts received from God; to work with order, peace, moderation, and patience, never shrinking from weariness and trials; to work above all with purity of intention and detachment from self, keeping unceasingly before my eyes death and the account that I must give of time lost, talents unused, good omitted, and vain complacency in success, so fatal to the work of God. All for Jesus, all through Mary, all after thy example, O Patriarch Joseph! Such shall be my watchword in life and death. Amen.

Litany of Humility

from Cardinal Rafael Merry de Val
O Jesus, meek and humble of heart, hear me!
From the desire of being esteemed, *deliver me, Jesus.*
From the desire of being loved, *deliver me, Jesus.*
From the desire of being extolled, *deliver me, Jesus.*

From the desire of being honored, *deliver me, Jesus.*
From the desire of being praised, *deliver me, Jesus.*
From the desire of being preferred to others, *deliver me, Jesus.*
From the desire of being consulted, *deliver me, Jesus.*
From the desire of being approved, *deliver me, Jesus.*
From the fear of being humiliated, *deliver me, Jesus.*
From the fear of being despised, *deliver me, Jesus.*
From the fear of suffering rebukes, *deliver me, Jesus.*
From the fear of being calumniated, *deliver me, Jesus.*
From the fear of being forgotten, *deliver me, Jesus.*
From the fear of being ridiculed, *deliver me, Jesus.*
From the fear of being wronged, *deliver me, Jesus.*
From the fear of being suspected, *deliver me, Jesus.*

That others may be loved more than I: *Jesus, grant me the grace to desire it.*
That others may be esteemed more than I: *Jesus, grant me the grace to desire it.*
That, in the opinion of the world, others may increase and I may decrease: *Jesus, grant me the grace to desire it.*
That others may be chosen and I set aside: *Jesus, grant me the grace to desire it.*
That others may be praised and I unnoticed: *Jesus, grant me the grace to desire it.*
That others may be preferred to me in everything: *Jesus, grant me the grace to desire it.*
That others may become holier than I, provided I become as holy as I should be, as holy as You want me to be, *Jesus, grant me the grace to desire it.*

For Single-mindedness in Prayer

A prayer to help you focus amid the many distractions in this world.
One thing I ask of the Lord: this I seek: to dwell in the house of the Lord all the days of my life—that I may gaze upon the loveliness of the Lord and contemplate His holy temple. (Psalm 27:4)

Surrender Prayer

I've found this simple prayer powerful when prayed in times of stress.
Jesus, Mary, and Joseph, I surrender myself to You with all that I am and have. Please take care of everything.

Entrustment to God the Father

Simple but helpful to pray and encourage others in times of worry.
Our Heavenly Father loves us, and He takes care of us.
My Heavenly Father loves me, and He takes care of me.

The Prayer of Job

I have prayed this prayer when death and great loss have come unexpectedly, using the words of the patriarch who blessed God even in the midst of his misery.
The LORD has given; the LORD has taken away.
Blessed be the Name of the LORD!

Prayer of Spiritual Communion

I'm grateful when I am able to attend daily Mass, but when I cannot attend Mass or, if attending, am unable to receive communion, I have found this prayer to be helpful:

My Jesus, I believe that You are present in the Most Holy Sacrament. I love You above all things, and I desire to receive You into my soul. Since I cannot now receive You sacramentally, come at least spiritually into my heart. I embrace You as if You were already come and unite myself wholly to You. Never permit me to be separated from You. Amen.

Seven Sorrows of Our Lady

I began praying these prayers on the recommendation of a Dominican priest and exorcist after relating to him a number of sorrowful incidents that had happened in my life. The many promised graces of this devotion include peace to the families of those who pray it, consolation in pain, and spiritual protection.

1. The Prophecy of Simeon: *"And Simeon blessed them and said to Mary his mother: Behold this child is set for the fall and for the resurrection of many in Israel, and for a sign which shall be contradicted; And thy own soul a sword shall pierce, that out of many hearts thoughts may be revealed." Luke 2: 34-35*

How great was the shock to Mary's Heart at hearing the sorrowful words, in which holy Simeon told the bitter Passion and death of her sweet Jesus, since in that same moment she realized in her mind all the insults, blows, and torments which the impious men were to offer to the Redeemer of the world. But a still sharper sword pierced her soul. It was the thought of men's ingratitude to her beloved Son. Now consider that because of your sins you are unhappily among the ungrateful. *Hail Mary…*

2. The flight into Egypt: *"And after they (the wise men) were departed, behold an angel of the Lord appeared in sleep to Joseph, saying: Arise and take the child and His mother and fly into Egypt: and be there until I shall tell thee. For it will come to pass that Herod will seek the child to destroy Him. Who arose and took the child and His mother by night and retired into Egypt: and He was there until the death of Herod." Matthew 2:13-14*

Consider the sharp sorrow which Mary felt when, St. Joseph being warned by an angel, she had to flee by night in order to preserve her beloved Child from the slaughter decreed by Herod. What anguish was hers, in leaving Judea, lest she should be overtaken by the soldiers of the cruel king! How great her privations in that long journey! What sufferings she bore in that land of exile, what sorrow amid that people given to idolatry! But consider how often you have renewed that bitter grief of Mary, when your sins have caused her Son to flee from your heart. *Hail Mary…*

3. The loss of the Child Jesus in the temple: *"And having fulfilled the days, when they returned, the Child Jesus remained in Jerusalem; and His parents knew it not. And thinking that he was in the company, they came a day's journey and sought him among their kinsfolk and acquaintance. And not finding Him, they returned to Jerusalem, seeking Him." Luke 2: 43-45*

How dread was the grief of Mary when she saw that she had lost her beloved Son! And as if to increase her sorrow, when she sought Him diligently among her kinsfolk and acquaintance, she could hear no tidings of Him. No hindrances stayed her, nor weariness, nor danger; but she forthwith returned to Jerusalem, and for three long days sought Him sorrowing. Great be your confusion, O my soul, who has so often lost your Jesus by your sins and has given no heed to seek Him at once, a sign that you make very little or no account of the precious treasure of divine love. *Hail Mary…*

4. The meeting of Jesus and Mary on the Way of the Cross: *"And there followed Him a great multitude of people, and of women, who bewailed and lamented Him." Luke 23: 27*

Come, O ye sinners, come and see if ye can endure so sad a sight. This Mother, so tender and loving, meets her beloved Son, meets Him amid an impious rabble, who drag Him to a cruel death, wounded, torn by stripes, crowned with thorns, streaming with blood, bearing His heavy cross. Ah, consider, my soul, the grief of the blessed Virgin thus beholding her Son! Who would not weep at seeing this Mother's grief? But who has been the cause of such woe? I, it is I, who with my sins have so cruelly wounded the heart of my sorrowing Mother! And yet I am not moved; I am as a stone, when my heart should break because of my ingratitude. *Hail Mary…*

5. The Crucifixion: *"They crucified Him… Now there stood by the cross of Jesus, His Mother. When Jesus therefore had seen His Mother and the disciple standing whom he loved, He said to His Mother: Woman: behold thy son. After that he said to the disciple: Behold thy Mother." John 19: 18, 25-27*

Look, devout soul, look to Calvary, whereon are raised two altars of sacrifice, one on the body of Jesus, the other on the heart of Mary. Sad is the sight of that dear Mother drowned in a sea of woe, seeing her beloved Son, part of her very self, cruelly nailed to the shameful tree of the cross. Ah me! how every blow of the hammer, how every stripe which fell on the Savior's form, fell also on the disconsolate spirit of the Virgin. As she stood at the foot of the cross, pierced by the sword of sorrow, she turned her eyes on Him, until she knew that He lived no longer and had resigned His spirit to His Eternal Father. Then her own soul was like to have left the body and joined itself to that of Jesus. *Hail Mary...*

6. The taking down of the Body of Jesus from the Cross: *"Joseph of Arimathea, a noble counselor, came and went in boldly to Pilate, and begged the body of Jesus. And Joseph buying fine linen, and taking Him down, wrapped Him up in the fine linen."* Mark 15: 43-46.

Consider the most bitter sorrow which rent the soul of Mary, when she saw the dead body of her dear Jesus on her knees, covered with blood, all torn with deep wounds. O mournful Mother, a bundle of myrrh, indeed, is thy Beloved to thee. Who would not pity thee? Whose heart would not be softened, seeing affliction which would move a stone? Behold John not to be comforted, Magdalen and the other Mary in deep affliction, and Nicodemus, who can scarcely bear his sorrow. *Hail Mary...*

7. The burial of Jesus: *"Now there was in the place where He was crucified, a garden; and in the garden a new sepulcher, wherein no man yet had been laid. There, therefore, because of the Passover of the Jews, they laid Jesus, because the sepulcher was nigh at hand." John 19: 41-42*

Consider the sighs which burst from Mary's sad heart when she saw her beloved Jesus laid within the tomb. What grief was hers when she saw the stone lifted to cover that sacred tomb! She gazed a last time on the lifeless body of her Son and could scarce detach her eyes from those gaping wounds. And when the great stone was rolled to the door of the sepulcher, oh, then indeed her heart seemed torn from her body! *Hail Mary…*

Let us pray: Most holy Virgin and Mother, whose soul was pierced by a sword of sorrow in the Passion of Thy divine Son, and who in His glorious Resurrection was filled with never-ending joy at His triumph; obtain for us who call upon Thee, so to be partakers in the adversities of Holy Church and the sorrows of the Sovereign Pontiff, as to be found worthy to rejoice with them in the consolations for which we pray, in the charity and peace of the same Christ our Lord. Amen. Our Lady of Sorrows, pray for us.

Prayer of Our Lady of All Nations

This prayer is a useful grounding, especially after the daily news.

Lord Jesus Christ, Son of the Father, send now Your Spirit over the earth. Let the Holy Spirit live in the hearts of all nations, that they may be preserved from degeneration, disaster, and war. May the Lady of all Nations, the Blessed Virgin Mary, be our Advocate. Amen.

Prayer to Make Up for Daily Neglects

I found this prayer in the Pieta book, which told the story of how it enabled the nun who prayed it nightly to enter heaven without any purgatory. It helps me to place all my confidence in Jesus to make up for my own personal failings and anything lacking in my actions as a husband and father. Pray a Glory Be *after each of the petitions.*

Eternal Father, in union with the Immaculate Heart of Mary, I offer You the Sacred Heart of Jesus, with all its love, all its sufferings and all its merits.

First, to expiate all the sins I have committed this day and during all my life. *Glory be...*

Second, to purify the good I have done badly this day and during all my life. *Glory Be...*

Third, to supply for the good I ought to have done and have neglected this day and during all my life. *Glory Be...*

Healing Prayer before Sleep

Sometimes when preparing for sleep and troubled in my mind from memories of past relationship issues or incidents, I have prayed this prayer which I adapted from a spiritual warfare ministry.

Jesus, through the power of the Holy Spirit, go back into my memory as I sleep. Every hurt that has ever been done to me—please heal that hurt. Every hurt that I have ever caused to another person—please heal that hurt. All of the relationships that have been damaged in my whole life—

please heal those relationships. And Lord, if there is anything I need to do—please guide me to do it. I choose to forgive and I ask to be forgiven. Remove whatever bitterness that may be in my heart, Lord, and fill the empty spaces with Your love. Thank You, Jesus! Amen.

Prayer to St. Joseph for Employment

Having been through four years of under-employment and falling into debt while trying to provide for my family, I thought it would be appropriate to include a prayer for those husbands and fathers who are struggling to find gainful employment. Whatever anxiety, discouragement, and feelings of failure you may be experiencing, I want to encourage you to turn more and more to deep daily prayer—especially the Rosary, Eucharistic adoration, the sacrament of Confession, and the Psalms. Here is a psalm from the Liturgy of the Hours' Friday Night Prayer that particularly spoke to me during that period of my life, followed by a prayer to St. Joseph for gainful employment.

O Lord, the God of my salvation: I have cried in the day, and in the night before Thee.

Let my prayer come in before Thee: incline Thy ear to my petition.

For my soul is filled with evils: and my life hath drawn nigh to hell.

I am counted among them that go down to the pit: I am become as a man without help,

Free among the dead, like the slain sleeping in the sepulchers, whom Thou remember no more: and they are cast off from Thy hand.

They have laid me in the lower pit: in the dark places, and in the shadow of death.

Thy wrath is strong over me: and all Thy waves Thou hast brought in upon me.

Thou hast put away my acquaintance far from me: they have set me an abomination to themselves. I was delivered up, and came not forth:

My eyes languished through poverty. All the day I cried to Thee, O Lord: I stretched out my hands to Thee.

Wilt Thou show wonders to the dead? or shall physicians raise to life, and give praise to Thee?

Shall any one in the sepulcher declare Thy mercy: and Thy truth in destruction?

Shall Thy wonders be known in the dark; and Thy justice in the land of forgetfulness?

But I, O Lord, have cried to Thee: and in the morning my prayer shall prevent Thee.

Lord, why cast Thou off my prayer: why turn Thou away Thy face from me?

I am poor, and in labors from my youth: and being exalted have been humbled and troubled.

Thy wrath hath come upon me: and Thy terrors have troubled me.

They have come round about me like water all the day: they have compassed me about together.

Friend and neighbor Thou hast put far from me: and my acquaintance, because of misery.

Dear Saint Joseph, with the words "do not fear to take Mary your wife" God entrusted to your care the Blessed Virgin Mary and that which was conceived in her by the Holy Spirit, Jesus. You embraced the responsibility of providing for the well-being of Jesus and Mary through your work. Please look with compassion upon me in my anxiety as I struggle to support my family. I implore you to help me find gainful employment soon, so that this great burden of concern will be lifted from my heart and that I may be able to adequately provide for those whom God has entrusted to my care. Guard me against discouragement, so that I may emerge from this trial spiritually enriched and with even greater blessings from God and a heart full of gratitude. Thank you, St. Joseph. Amen.

2

the father who prays with his wife

"The husband and wife who pray together stay together."

"Likewise you husbands, live considerately with your wives, bestowing honor on the woman as the weaker sex, since you are joint heirs of the grace of life, in order that your prayers may not be hindered."
1 Peter 3:7

Fr. Peyton's famous saying "The family that prays together stays together" I have adapted to: "The husband and wife who pray together stay together." If the husband and wife stay together, the family is more likely to stay together. In addition to that we have Jesus' promise that:

> ...if two of you shall consent upon earth, concerning anything whatsoever they shall ask, it shall be done to them by my Father who is in

heaven. For where there are two or three gathered together in My name, there am I in the midst of them. (Matthew 18:19-20)

This makes the sacrament of marriage the fountain of grace for the family…because there are two people (hopefully three or more later on!) together in Jesus' name.

Remember the command given to the first priest ever, Adam, to "till and keep the garden," which contained the "crown of creation," the wife specially created for him by God, Eve. It would seem that it was Adam's failure to "keep the garden"—including his wife—from spiritual danger that led to the downfall of the human race. Let us not neglect spousal prayer to the detriment and downfall of our own marriages and families.

Praying together as a couple on a daily basis is necessary. This may be short, just a brief joining of hands and offering in the morning, evening, or whenever you can snatch a moment, but try to do at least something like that. Especially during times of tension in the marriage, commit to praying together.

When children come into the marriage, it can be easy to forget about your marriage in the activity of caring for children. In the throes of busy family life, it may sometimes happen that you are praying as a family together with the children, but not together as a couple. Remember that the grace to parent your children comes through your marriage. I encourage you to keep trying to return to praying together as a couple. Renew your love for one another, and you will find the grace to face any parenting difficulties together.

After God and my own salvation, I have to recognize that my marriage should always be my first concern. Am I loving my wife as myself? Is my wife happy? Am I caring for her needs? Am I providing for her? Am I praying, fasting, and offering sacrifices on her behalf so that she will be strengthened, encouraged, and protected in her daily duties as a wife and mother?

Christ said that any man who wishes to be His disciple must deny himself, take up his cross daily and follow Him. So you must embrace your cross daily.

Try this exercise, which I gave to my eldest goddaughter and her husband to do at their wedding reception. You and your wife face each other. Hold your arms out like Jesus on the cross. Look at each other. You are now each looking at your daily cross. Now embrace your cross...daily. Follow Jesus all the way to heaven.

Renewal of marriage vows

We have found it fitting to renew our marriage vows in the presence of our children on anniversaries (or even monthly), to remind ourselves of what we vowed to do. So here are the Catholic wedding vows. Don't forget them! Remember, remember, remember your wedding vows!

Groom: I, _____, take you, _____, for my lawful wife, to have and to hold from this day forward, for better for worse, for richer, for poorer, in sickness and in health, till death do us part.

Bride: I, _____, take you, _____, for my lawful husband, to have and to hold from this day forward, for better for worse, for richer, for poorer, in sickness and in health, till death do us part.

A married couple's consecration to the Holy Family

On a retreat the weekend before our marriage, I composed the following prayer. My bride and I prayed this prayer together on the day of our marriage and have been blessed to be able to renew it every month. We're offering it here as an example of one you and your wife might want to make for yourself. As we both had given our lives to Christ and had devotions to Mary and St. Joseph, it seemed fitting to consecrate our new family to the Holy Family.

Jesus, Mary, and Joseph, graciously accept us and our marriage which we dedicate and consecrate to you this day.

Holy Family, we desire to model our marriage and family life according to your own. Show us how to be patient and kind in dealing with each other's shortcomings, for no one is without them. May we be slow to speak harshly and quick to forgive each other. Make us true and affectionate, eager to please, and ready to deny our own will and inclination in all things, so that we may be of one heart and one mind in Christ. Help us to imitate your holy life at Nazareth—to be simple, prayerful, and peace-loving, helpful to our neighbors, patient in bearing the trials and crosses of this life, and solicitous about setting a good example in our community.

Lord Jesus Christ, grant that both of us may constantly and earnestly strive to lead a perfect Christian life, so that the divine image of Your mystical union with Holy Church, imprinted upon us on the happy day of our marriage, may shine forth more and more clearly.

Mary, ever-virgin Mother of Jesus, we ask through Your intercession to be blessed with holy children. We desire to receive them with love and gratitude from God as His supreme gift to marriage and as a manifestation of our marriage union. Help us to bring them up in the love and law of Christ as reveal through His Holy Church.

St. Joseph, virgin-father of our Savior, guardian of His Holy Mother, head of the Holy Family, assist us by your prayers in all our spiritual and temporal needs. Help us to imitate your great humility and service to Our Lord Jesus Christ and His Immaculate Mother. Pray that we may be kept free from being selfish, competitive, or entrapped by material possessions and concerns.

Holy Family, please accept this our act of consecration, and keep the memory of it alive in our hearts each day of our lives, so that we may be found worthy by the help of

God's grace to be taken to heaven, there to be joined by our children forever to praise and thank God with all the holy angels and saints for all eternity, Amen.

Prayer for the marriage bed

Holy angels and saints, please watch over and protect our marriage bed.

Prayer for conception

O Father God,

You bade the first man and woman to be fruitful and multiply, so we ask You to hear the prayer of our hearts and if it be Your holy will, grant our desire for a child, as You heard the prayers of Rachel, Hannah, Anne, and Elizabeth.

Guide us in all our choices so that this conception, pregnancy, and birth are in line with Your will. Thank you for hearing the prayers of our hearts and guide us in our actions through Your Son Jesus Christ, Who lives and reigns with You and the Holy Spirit, one God forever and ever. Amen.

Prayer for the expansion of the family

Sometimes it can be hard to be open to life, especially when difficulties are present. Here is a simple prayer composed by Steve Wood which my wife and I have prayed together.

Lord God, if You would like us to have another child, please put that desire in our hearts.

Prayer for a healthy pregnancy

Heavenly Father, molder of body and soul, thank You for the gift of life that You have placed in my wife's womb. Thank you, Lord, for sending this child to my wife and me. Father, give us the grace to be good parents and help us to bring up this child in a way that brings glory to Your Name. Be a shield of protection around this child as he or she develops in my wife's womb. Protect my wife from every manner of sickness and disease to which pregnant women are vulnerable and grant her peace and trust in Your provision. Blessed Virgin Mary, you carried Jesus, the Son of God, in your immaculate womb for nine months, nurturing and caring for Him most perfectly. Please allow me to entrust the child in my wife's womb to your care.

Litany of saints for childbirth

My wife has benefitted from this litany, composed by a friend of hers. Each of these saints has traditionally been invoked during different stages of pregnancy, labor, and after the baby is born.

1. Invoking the patrons of expectant mothers:
   Saints Anne and Elizabeth … pray for us
   Saint Anthony of Padua …
   St. Margaret of Antioch…
   St. Gerard Majella…
   St. Ulric…
   St. Joseph, Guardian of the Redeemer…
   All you holy men and women, pray for us!

2. Invoking patrons of labor and childbirth:
    St. Leonard of Noblac…
    St. Eramsus of Formia …
    St. Lutgarde of Aywières…
    St. Margaret of Fontana…
    Our Lady, Blessed Mother…
    All you holy men and women, pray for us!

3. Invoking protection against hemorrhage,
    ruptures, extreme pain and prolonged suffering:
    St. Lucy of Syracuse…
    Sts. Drogo and Florentius …
    Sts. Osmund and Madron …
    St. Charles Borremeo …
    All you holy men and women, pray for us!

4. Invoking holy women of great insight
    St. Hildegard of Bingen…
    St. Teresa of Avila …
    Sts. Cecelia and Catherine…
    St. Kateri Tekawitha…
    St. Elizabeth Ann Seton …
    St. Edith Stein…
    All you holy men and women, pray for us!

5. Invoking patrons of newborn infants:
    St. Philomena …
    St. Brigid of Ireland …
    St. Zeno of Verona …
    St. Nicholas …
    St. Philip Neri…
    All the Holy Innocents…

6. Invoking patrons of nursing and healing mothers:
   St. Martina…
   St. Concordia …
   Saints Joachim and Joseph …
   St. Cadoc…
   St. Pancras …
   Our Lady of La Leche…
   All you holy men and women, pray for us!

Prayer for our children's future spouses

Lord, please prepare our children for their vocation and help us, their parents, to do whatever is needed to help them in this calling. If they are to be married, please be working in the hearts and lives of their spouses now to prepare them for their future marriage and to draw them close to You and Your blessed Mother. Amen.

Prayer for religious vocations

O God, grant that one of our children or grandchildren may become a faithful, fervent priest or religious. We want to live as good Christians and want to guide our children always to do what is right and pleasing to You. May we receive this grace, O God, to be allowed to give you a holy priest or religious! Amen.

3

the father who blesses his family

"The blessings of your father are mighty beyond the blessings of the eternal mountains, the bounties of the everlasting hills."
Genesis 49:26

In the book of Numbers 6:22-27, God told Moses how the priests were to bless the people of Israel so that His Name would be upon them and He would bless them. We fathers can imitate this by taking time to regularly bless our children, especially during significant moments or when they are facing trials. Blessing our families is both necessary and powerful. Fathers of families, as representatives of God the Father, have authority to call down God's blessing on wife and children. Let us not neglect this. Let us leave them in no doubt of our love and God's love for them.

In Matthew 3:17, God the Father set us an example of expressing this love when He called from heaven at Jesus' baptism saying, "This is My beloved Son, in Whom I am well pleased." God the Father reiterated this at Jesus' Transfiguration shortly before He went to Jerusalem to endure His Passion and Crucifixion.

Gently tracing the Sign of the Cross † on the foreheads of your wife and children with holy water or holy oil when giving these blessings is an apropos gesture to include as a means of putting Christ's Name on them so that He will bless and protect them.

The call to prayer

When gathering the family for prayer, you can use this traditional prayer and response as a means of making them aware that prayer has begun. If they are already present, you can use it as the opening for the main prayer or blessing.

L. Our help is in the name of the Lord.
R. Who has made heaven and earth.
L: The Lord be with you.
R: And with your spirit.

Blessing of children & family members

Based on Numbers 6:24-26

May the Lord bless you and keep you. May the Lord make His face shine upon you and be gracious to you. May the Lord lift up His countenance to you and give you His peace.

And may the Lord bless you † in the Name of the Father, and of the Son, and of the Holy Spirit. Amen.

I composed this prayer based on Acts 2:17-18:
O God, pour out Your Spirit upon all flesh: on our sons and on our daughters, and on our young men and on our old men, and on Your servants and on Your handmaidens, pour out You Spirit. Amen.

Blessing for a departing child/guest
A traditional Irish blessing at the parting of ways
May the road rise up to meet you. May the wind be always at your back. May the sun shine warm upon your face; the rains fall soft upon your fields, and until we meet again, may God hold you in the palm of His hand.
O Almighty and merciful God, Who has commissioned Your angels to guide and protect us, command them to be our assiduous companions from our setting out until our return; to clothe us with their invisible protection; to keep from us all danger of collision, of fire, of explosion, of fall and bruises, and finally, having preserved us from all evil, and especially from sin, to guide us to our heavenly home. Through Jesus Christ, our Lord. Amen.

Prayer for a sick child/family member
Almighty and Eternal God, You are the everlasting health of those who believe in You. Hear our prayers for Your sick servant (N...) for whom we implore the aid of Your tender mercy, that being restored to bodily health, he (she) may give thanks to You in Your Church.

Through Christ our Lord. Amen.

St. Raphael, patron angel of health and healing, pray for us!

Prayer for children against nightmares

Adapted from Catholic.net.

Dear Lord Jesus, as my child rests in the comfort of Your love, I ask that they may experience Your gentle embrace and care. I entrust them to Your compassionate care to bring peace to their mind, serenity to their heart and renewal to their spirit. O Jesus Savior, in Your loving compassion, I ask that you grant my child a peaceful night's rest. Please purify their dreams, cleanse their subconscious and wash their thoughts with the purity of your infinite love. Please send forth Your protective angels to stand guard over them as they sleep. May Your angelic army destroy anything that might have been sent against their ability to experience a peaceful night's rest. I ask that St. Raphael and their guardian angel surround them as they sleep, that awake they may keep watch with Christ, and asleep, rest in His peace. Amen.

Saint Raphael travel prayer

We pray this beloved prayer when beginning long trip: Saint Raphael is the hero of the biblical Book of Tobit and also happens to be the patron of courtship and finances, so we have asked for his intercession when we or family members have concerns in those areas as well.

O Saint Raphael, patron angel of travelers and happy meetings, lead us by the hand towards those we are looking for. May all our movements and all their movements be guided by your light and transfigured by your joy. Angel guide of Tobias, lay the request we now address to you at the feet of Him on Whose unveiled face you are privileged to gaze: *(here mention the intention: for safe journeys and happy meetings, etc.)* Lonely and tired, crushed by the separations and sorrows of earth, we feel the need of calling upon you and pleading for the protection of your wings, so that we may not be strangers in the province of joy and ignorant of the concerns of our country. Remember the weak, you who are strong, you whose home lies beyond the region of thunder in a land that is always peaceful, always serene, and bright with the resplendent glory of God.

Our Father… Hail Mary… Glory Be…

Saint Raphael, patron angel of travelers, pray for us!

Prayer for study and students

During college and as a married graduate student, I had this prayer (attributed to St. Thomas Aquinas) on a plaque. I prayed it from time to time during my academic studies.

Creator of all things, true source of Light and Wisdom, lofty Source of all Being, graciously let a ray of Your Brilliance penetrate into the darkness of my understanding and take from me the double darkness into which I have been born: an obscurity of both sin and ignorance.

Give me a sharp sense of understanding, a retentive memory, and the ability to grasp things correctly and fundamentally. Grant me the talent of being exact in my explanations and the ability to express myself with thoroughness and charm. Point out the beginning, direct the progress, and set Your seal upon the finished work. Through Christ Our Lord. Amen.

Prayer of a child for their future spouse

During times when our youth are longing to meet that special someone, encourage them to pray this prayer.

O Jesus, lover of the young, the dearest Friend I have, in all confidence I open my heart to You to beg Your light and assistance in the important task of planning my future. Give me the light of Your grace, that I may decide wisely concerning the person who is to be my partner through life. Dearest Jesus, send me such a one whom in Your divine wisdom You judge best suited to be united with me in marriage. May her/his character reflect some of the traits of Your own Sacred Heart. May s/he be upright, loyal, pure, sincere and noble, so that with united efforts and with pure and unselfish love we both may strive to perfect ourselves in soul and body, as well as the children it may please You to entrust to our care. Bless our friendship before marriage, that sin may have no part in it. May our mutual love bind us so closely that our future home may ever be most like Your own at Nazareth.

O Mary Immaculate, sweet Mother of the young, to your special care I entrust the decision I am to make as to my future wife/husband. You are my guiding Star! Direct me to the person with whom I can best cooperate in doing

God's Holy Will, with whom I can live in peace, love and harmony in this life, and attain to eternal joys in the next. Amen.

Prayer of a child to know their vocation

When your child is not sure what God is calling them to, here is a prayer for them to know their vocation. Adapted from KolbeCenter.org.

For a young man:

St. Joseph, God made me out of love and He has a special plan for my life. From the beginning He made us male and female. As a man, I know that God created me to serve Him and my brothers and sisters either as a priest, as a religious brother, as a husband and father, or, as a consecrated single man in the world so that I can carry out a special mission for Him. On my behalf, please ask Him to show me which of these paths He wants me to take. Please help me to be pure and chaste, practice respectful manners, to save myself for the mission God has for me so that I can give of myself completely. Thank you, St. Joseph. Amen.

For a young woman:

Blessed Virgin Mary, God made me out of love and He has a special plan for my life. From the beginning He made us male and female. As a woman, I know that God has created me to serve Him and my brothers and sisters as a nun or religious sister, as a wife and mother, or, to be single in the world so that I can carry out a special mission for Him there. On my behalf, please ask Him to show me which of these paths He wants me to take. Please help me to be pure and chaste, to dress modestly, to save myself for the mission God has for me so that I can give of myself completely. Thank you, Blessed Mother Mary. Amen.

4

the father who blesses his home

"My house is the house of prayer." Luke 19:46

"Be you also as living stones built up, a spiritual house, a holy priesthood, to offer up spiritual sacrifices, acceptable to God by Jesus Christ." 1 Peter 2:5

"For we know, if our earthly house of this habitation be dissolved, that we have a building of God, a house not made with hands, eternal in heaven." 2 Corinthians 5:1

While Catholic priests and deacons offer formal blessings, laypeople can give blessings that invoke God's protection and blessing in daily life.

Holy water is helpful to have on hand for blessings. Most of the following blessings include the sprinkling of holy water, for example, on the doorways, windows, and furniture of a room, or on the animal or vehicle being blessed. Be sure to always have some in your home.

Blessing a house

I recommend having your house formally blessed by an ordained priest. The following prayers can be used as a renewal of the formal blessing.
O heavenly Father, Almighty God, we humbly beseech Thee to bless and sanctify this house and all who dwell therein and everything else in it, and do Thou vouchsafe to fill it with all good things; grant to them, O Lord, the abundance of heavenly blessings and from the richness of the earth every substance necessary for life, and finally direct their desires to the fruits of Thy mercy. At our entrance, therefore, deign to bless and sanctify this house as Thou didst deign to bless the house of Abraham, of Isaac, and of Jacob; and may the angels of Thy light, dwelling within the walls of this house, protect it and those who dwell therein. Through Christ our Lord. Amen.

Blessing a home

I recently found this prayer on a plaque in a thrift shop. I liked it so much that I bought the plaque for the home of my recently married daughter and her husband.
Bless, O Lord, Almighty God, this home, that here there may be health, chastity, prosperity, humility, goodness, meekness, obedience, and thanksgiving to God the Father, Son, and Holy Spirit. May God's blessing remain upon this

home and upon those dwelling here. Through Christ our Lord. Amen.

Home consecration

This prayer was composed by a friend and mentor of mine, and my wife and I pray it monthly.

Most Blessed Virgin, whose heart is sorrowful and immaculate, we recognize thee as the Lady and Queen of this house. Have the kindness to preserve it from any evil: from fire, water, thunder, storms, earthquakes, from robbers, wicked people, from revolutionaries, war, raids, from persecutions and taxes, from any other evil known to thee. Bless, protect, defend, and preserve as thy personal property those who live and will live here. Keep them away from adversity and misfortune, but above all, preserve them from offending God. Let not a single mortal sin be ever committed in this house and may all those who enter it work for the glory of God, for the reign of Jesus and Mary.

Blessing a bedroom

Bless this bedroom, Lord, so that all who occupy it may remain firm in Your peace and purity. May they persevere in Your will and so come to that eternal rest in Your kingdom of heaven. Through Christ our Lord. Amen.

Blessing of a new vehicle

Lend a willing ear, Lord God, to our prayers, and bless this vehicle with Your holy right hand. Direct Your holy angels to accompany it, that they may protect those who ride in it from all dangers and always guard them. And just as by Your deacon Philip You gave faith and grace to the man of Ethiopia as he sat in his chariot reading the Sacred Word, so, point out to Your servants the way of salvation. Grant that, aided by Your grace, and with their hearts set on good works, they may, after all the joys and sorrows of this journey through life, merit to receive eternal joys, through Christ our Lord. Amen.

Blessings of a new pet/farm animal

Following are options for blessing pets or farm animals. At the end of each prayer, you may bless the animal(s) with holy water.

1. Lord Jesus Christ, Our God and King of heaven and earth, You are the Word of the Father by Whom all creatures were created and given to us for our support. Look down, we beseech You, on our lowliness. As You have given us these animals as our companions and to assist us in our needs, so in Your great goodness, bless, guard and preserve them. While You give us temporal blessings through them, may You grant us continual graces so that we may all praise Your holy name forever. Amen.

2. A reading from the book of Genesis:
[In the beginning,] God said, "Let the water teem with an abundance of living creatures, and on the earth let birds fly beneath the dome of the sky." And so it happened: God created the great sea monsters and all kinds of swimming creatures with which the water teems, and all kinds of

winged birds. God saw how good it was, and God blessed them, saying, "Be fertile, multiply, and fill the water of the seas; and let the birds multiply on the earth.: Evening came and morning followed: the fifth day.

Then God said, "Let the earth bring forth all kinds of living creatures: cattle, creeping things, and wild animals of all kinds." And so it happened: God made all kinds of wild animals, all kinds of cattle, and all kinds of creeping things of the earth. God saw how good it was. (Genesis 1:20-25)
The Word of the Lord.
R. Thanks be to God.

O God, You have done all things wisely; in Your goodness You have made us in Your image and given us care over other living things. Reach out with Your right hand and grant that these animals may serve our needs and that Your bounty in the resources of this life may move us to seek more confidently the goal of eternal life. We ask this through Christ our Lord. Amen.

(Here the animals may be sprinkled with holy water.)

3. May these animals, Lord, receive Your blessing. Keep them sound in body, and through the intercession of St. Anthony the Hermit, St. Isidore the Farmer, and St. Francis of Assisi, may they be freed from every evil, through Christ our Lord. Amen.

Pet/animal funeral prayers

Having been called upon to preside at the burial of more than a few dead pets and various deceased wild creatures, I have found the funeral blessings for animals to be a helpful accessory in the toolkit of a domestic priest. This prayer is based on one written by Maria Paola Daud and Kathleen N. Hattrup.

Lord God, we thank you for the gift of (pet's name or type of animal). With St. Francis, we pray: "Be praised, my Lord, through all Your creatures." As the Scripture says, "For You love all things that exist, and detest none of the things that You have made; for You would not have made anything if You had hated it." (Wisdom 11:24)

We know that every creature is loved by You and part of Your design for the world. For You give each living thing a place in creation, and even the fleeting existence of the least of them is given Your love and affection.

(If the deceased is a pet) Lord God, our affection for *(pet's name)* thus reminds us of You. Thank You for the time that we have had with them. Thank You for making us the steward of their existence. Thank You for the joy that they have brought us. May all of creation always lead us to praise You and love You more, Father, Son, and Holy Spirit. Amen.

Blessing of the garden

Adapted from the Rural Life Prayerbook.

Almighty and most merciful God, before our first parents, Adam and Eve, sinned, they lived and were very happy in the Garden of Eden. There, as we read in the Holy Book, You would walk with them "in the cool of the day," and they heard the sound of You in the garden. Later, Your own Son, our Lord Jesus Christ began His fearful passion with His sweat of blood in the Garden of Gethsemane. Dear God, ever since then, a garden is a holy place. You still walk there with men, in the cool of the day. You walk with men who can see You and Your generous and merciful providence working for them in the green things that grow and the trees that blossom and bear such rich and nourishing fruit: men who can see again the cross of Christ in every tree, and His crown of thorns in every thorn.

Bless all our gardens and orchards in this broad land of ours, dear God, and give us a rich and plentiful harvest. Help us, as we go about our work here, to see You in Your loving kindness, working for us and with us. Help us to do Your will at all times so that someday we will walk with You and Your Son and our dear Mother Mary down the paths of another Garden, far better and more beautiful than even the Garden of Eden. Amen.

Blessing of the harvest

Another gem from the Rural Life Prayerbook.

Almighty Lord God, You keep on giving abundance to men in the dew of heaven, and food out of the richness of the soil. We give thanks to Your most gracious majesty for the fruits of the field which we have gathered. We beg of You, in Your mercy, to bless our harvest, which we have received from Your generosity. Preserve it and keep it from all harm. Grant, too, that all those whose desires You have filled with these good things may be happy in Your protection. May they praise Your mercies forever and make use of the good things that do not last in such a way that they may not lose those goods that are everlasting, through Christ our Lord. Amen.

Blessing of the bacon (or other homegrown food)

Bless, O Lord, this bacon (or other food), that it may be an effective remedy for the human race, and grant that through the invocation of Thy holy Name all those who eat of it may obtain health of body and protection of their souls. Through Christ our Lord. Amen.

Blessed are You, O Lord, our God, Who has declared all foods clean!

Toasts and Thanksgiving

When drinking wine:

L: Blessed are You, Lord our God, King of the Universe, Who has created the fruit of the vine.

R: Jesus, meek and humble of heart, make our hearts like unto Thine.

When drinking hard cider or another fruit alcohol:

L: Blessed are You, Lord our God, King of the Universe, Who has created the fruit of the tree.

R: Jesus, meek and humble of heart, make our hearts like unto Thee.

Upon eating the first slice of homemade or special bread:
L: Blessed are You, Lord our God, King of the Universe, Who bring forth bread from the earth.
R: And thank You, Father, for Your Son, Jesus Christ, and blessed be His birth.

5

the father as teacher of prayer

"Lord, teach us to pray…" Luke 11:1

The domestic priest is the "master catechist" of his family. This portion of a homily to fathers from St. John Chrysostom lays out how this can happen after Sunday Mass:

> …when you go home from [Mass], lay out with your meal a spiritual meal as well. The father of the family might repeat something of what was said here; his wife could then hear it, the children too could learn something, and even the servants might be instructed. In short, the household might become a church, so that the devil is driven off and that evil spirit, the enemy of our salvation, takes to flight; the grace of the Holy Spirit would rest there instead, and all peace and harmony would surround the inhabitants. (*Second Sermon on Genesis*)

A good Jewish father like St. Joseph was called to teach his son the Law and a trade, and that includes teaching his children prayers. While the mother may actually do the teaching as a miniature *Mater Ecclesia*, the father can ensure that the child knows the prayers and can pray them, especially when preparing for receiving the sacraments.

First prayers and favorite prayers

These are the first prayers children learn and are the basis for so much else in the Catholic life. These prayers are reproduced here for simplicity's sake. Some families pray them in Latin or in their ancestral language as well. If the prayers are prayed in a group, the response is noted with an R. The first of these are the prayers which are used in the Rosary. The Latin versions are included as well.

Our Father, Who art in heaven, hallowed be Thy name. Thy kingdom come; Thy will be done on earth as it is in heaven.

R: Give us this day our daily bread, and forgive us our trespasses, as we forgive those who trespass against us, and lead us not into temptation, but deliver us from evil. Amen.

PATER NOSTER, qui es in caelis,
sanctificetur nomen tuum. Adveniat regnum tuum.
Fiat voluntas tua, sicut in caelo et in terra.
R: Panem nostrum quotidianum da nobis hodie, et dimitte
nobis debita nostra sicut et nos dimittimus debitoribus
nostris. Et ne nos inducas in tentationem, sed libera nos a
malo. Amen.

Hail Mary, full of grace, the Lord is with thee!
Blessed art thou among women, and blessed is the fruit of
thy womb, Jesus.
R: Holy Mary, Mother of God, pray for us sinners now
and at the hour of our death. Amen.

AVE MARIA, gratia plena, Dominus tecum.
Benedicta tu in mulieribus, et benedictus fructus ventris
tui, Iesus.
R: Sancta Maria, Mater Dei, ora pro nobis peccatoribus,
nunc, et in hora mortis nostrae. Amen.

Glory be to the Father, & to the Son, & to the Holy Spirit
R: As it was in the beginning, is now, and ever shall be,
world without end. Amen.

GLORIA PATRI, et Filio, et Spiritui Sancto.
R: Sicut erat in principio, et nunc, et semper, et in saecula
saeculorum. Amen.

Come Holy Spirit

*This ancient prayer is important for a child approaching confirmation
to learn and is particularly powerful for teens and young adults.*
Come, Holy Spirit, fill the hearts of Thy faithful
And enkindle in them the fire of Thy love.
Send forth Thy Spirit, and they shall be created
And Thou shalt renew the face of the earth.

Let us pray: O God, Who by the light of the Holy Spirit
did instruct the hearts of the faithful, grant that in the same
Spirit we may be truly wise, and ever rejoice in His
consolation, through Christ Our Lord, Amen.

The Confiteor

*This is prayed in the penitential rite at Mass, and when prayed
publicly, results in the forgiveness of all venial sin.*
I confess to almighty God and to you, my brothers and
sisters, that I have greatly sinned
in my thoughts and in my words,
in what I have done,
and in what I have failed to do; *(strike your breast 3X)*
through my fault, through my fault,
through my most grievous fault;
therefore I ask blessed Mary ever-Virgin,
all the Angels and Saints,
and you, my brothers and sisters,
to pray for me to the Lord our God.

Act of Contrition

Necessary for a child to learn when receiving the sacrament of Penance.
O my God, I am heartily sorry for having offended Thee,
and I detest all my sins because I dread the loss of heaven
and the pains of hell, but most of all because they offend
Thee, my God, Who are all-good and deserving of all my
love. I firmly resolve, with the help of Thy grace, to
confess my sins, do penance, and amend my life.

Act of Faith

O my God, I firmly believe that You are one God in three divine Persons, Father, Son, and Holy Spirit.

I believe that Your divine Son became man, died for our sins, rose again from the dead, ascended into heaven, and that He will come to judge the living and the dead.

I believe these and all the truths which the Holy Catholic Church teaches because You have revealed them Who are eternal truth and wisdom, Who can neither deceive nor be deceived.

In this faith I intend to live and die. Amen.

Act of Hope

O Lord God, I hope by Your grace for the pardon of all my sins and after life here to gain eternal happiness because You have promised it Who are infinitely powerful, faithful, kind, and merciful.

In this hope I intend to live and die. Amen.

Act of Love

O Lord God, I love You above all things and I love my neighbor for Your sake because You are the highest, infinite and perfect good, worthy of all my love.

In this love I intend to live and die. Amen.

Blessing Food at the Table

These are the standard blessings. You may choose to personalize them for your family by adding a prayer for the souls of the faithful departed (included here in the grace after meals) or for those suffering from hunger, as many families do.

Grace before Meals

Bless us, O Lord, and these Thy gifts, which we are about to receive from Thy bounty, through Christ, Our Lord. Amen.

Grace after Meals

We give Thee thanks for all Thy benefits, Almighty God, Who lives and reigns forever. May the souls of the faithful departed through the mercy of God rest in peace. Amen.

Personal Night Prayer for children

This is the version of a private night prayer that I have taught my children, starting when they were very young and adding more to it after they reached the age of reason:

- ❖ Act of Contrition *(Simplified for young children)*
- ❖ God bless … *(name each family member)*
- ❖ Angel of God
- ❖ End with a Hail Mary

Guardian Angel Prayers

One of these simple rhymed prayers can be prayed in the morning, and one—or both!—at night. Our own children usually love these prayers.

Angel of God, my guardian dear,
to whom God's love commits me here,
Ever this day/night, be at my side,
To light and guard, to rule and guide. Amen.

Good night, Guardian Angel,
The day has sped away;
Well spent or ill, its story is written down for aye.
Now, of God's kind Providence,
Thou image pure and bright,
watch over me while I'm sleeping.
My Angel dear, good night!

The Memorare Novena

Used by Mother Teresa as her go-to last resort, prayed nine times successively.

Remember, O most gracious Virgin Mary,
that never was it known that anyone who fled to thy protection,
implored thy help, or sought thy intercession was left unaided.
Inspired by this confidence,
I fly unto thee, O Virgin of virgins, my mother;
to thee do I come, before thee I stand, sinful and sorrowful.
O Mother of the Word Incarnate, despise not my petitions,
but in thy mercy, hear and answer me. Amen.

Memorare to St. Joseph

Remember, O most chaste spouse of the Blessed Virgin Mary, that never was it known,

that anyone who fled to thy protection, implored thy help, or sought thy intercession was left unaided.

Inspired by this confidence, I fly unto thee, O St. Joseph, Guardian of the Redeemer. O virgin father of our Savior, despise not my humble supplication, but in your bounty, hear and answer me. Amen.

Fatima Prayer to the Trinity

Most Holy Trinity, Father, Son and Holy Spirit, I adore Thee profoundly. I offer Thee the most precious Body, Blood, Soul and Divinity of Jesus Christ, present in all the tabernacles of the world, in reparation for the outrages, sacrileges and indifferences by which He is offended. And through the infinite merits of His Most Sacred Heart and the Immaculate Heart of Mary, I beg of Thee the conversion of poor sinners.

Incidental Prayers

Prayer can be a spiritual work of mercy and instructive to children when it is natural, instinctive, a habit, a way of life. Praying spontaneously on these occasions brings God back to mind amid the activities of the day.

Prayer when passing a church

St. Francis of Assisi prayed this as soon as he spotted the steeple of a church where Christ was present in the Eucharist:

L: We adore You, O Christ, and we praise You, here and
in all the tabernacles of the world
R: because by Your holy Cross, You have redeemed the
world.

Prayer when hearing a siren

*In first grade, my Dominican teacher Sister Victoria taught us to stop
whatever we were doing to pray a Hail Mary whenever we heard a siren,
whether it be from the police, fire department, or ambulance. I've taught
my children to do the same (and I usually also pray for the repose of the
soul of Sister Victoria):*
Hail Mary…
Lord, be with those concerned and may they do Your
Will. Amen.

Prayer when passing a place where
Christ is mocked

*We pray St. Maximilian Kolbe's prayer, taken from the Miraculous
Medal, when we pass a Freemasonic temple, an abortion clinic, a
"family planning" (contraceptive) center, pornographic establishment, or
occultic store or any other place where Our Lord is offended:*
O Mary conceived without sin, pray for us who have
recourse to thee! And for those who do not have recourse
to thee, especially _______ and those recommended to thee.

Prayer when passing a cemetery

This prayer comes from the great St. Bridget of Sweden and is said to release a soul from purgatory each time it is prayed: pray it frequently—daily—for your ancestors.

Eternal Father, I offer Thee the most precious Blood
of Thy divine Son, Jesus, in union with the Masses said
throughout the world today,
for all the holy souls in purgatory,
for sinners everywhere,
for sinners in the universal Church,
those in our own home and in our family. Amen.

Eternal rest grant unto them, O Lord, and let perpetual
light shine upon them. May their souls and the souls of all
the faithful departed, through the mercy of God, rest in
peace. Amen.

Prayer when making a sacrifice

This prayer comes from the apparitions of Fatima and is quite powerful, for both children and adults to pray when faced with some sacrifice, great or small:

Jesus, I offer this up for love of You, the conversion of
sinners, and in reparation for the sins committed against
the Immaculate Heart of Mary.

Prayer when something is lost

We usually at least pray the first couplet: St. Anthony has been very good to our family!

Dear St. Anthony, please come around,
for something is lost and cannot be found.

As the Good Shepherd searches out the lost sheep,
Find what we've lost and our soul to keep.
May we find God in the hidden place,
and when we die, behold His face.

The Divine Praises

Praising the LORD gives us joy and strength! On occasions where a father wants to lead the family in the praise of God to thank Him for a blessing or simply to express joy, there are few things better than the Divine Praises. The family can repeat each line after the father or can repeat the prayers together.

Blessed be God.
Blessed be His Holy Name.
Blessed be Jesus Christ, true God and true man.
Blessed be the Name of Jesus.
Blessed be his most Sacred Heart.
Blessed be his most Precious Blood.
Blessed be Jesus in the most holy Sacrament of the altar.
Blessed be the Holy Spirit, the Paraclete.
Blessed be the great Mother of God, Mary most holy.
Blessed be her holy and Immaculate Conception.
Blessed be her glorious Assumption.
Blessed be the name of Mary, Virgin and Mother.
Blessed be Saint Joseph, her most chaste Spouse.
Blessed be God in his Angels and in his Saints. Amen.

6

the father as leader of family prayer

"Have no anxiety about anything, but in everything by prayer and supplication with thanksgiving let your requests be made known to God." Philippians 4:6

Fathers, not mothers, should be the primary leaders of prayer in the family. It is important that men set the example for their family, especially their sons. Some men may find it challenging to lead their families in prayer, especially if they are married to a devout wife who has a heart for prayer. But one of the best gifts a husband can give his wife is to lead the family in prayer so that she doesn't have to. It is also useful to train your sons in how to pray and how to lead prayer. In a world that mocks piety, a man who is comfortable in leading prayer has an impact. In this section are some daily prayers of the Church, including the Canticles prayed in the Liturgy of the Hours morning, evening, and night. These canticles were all recorded by St. Luke in his Gospel, and they are a deliberate tying together of the Old and New Testaments, hence exemplative of our faith.

Morning Prayer

There are many ways to lead morning prayers, and this is something that will be specific to each family. A formal morning prayer service can consist of singing a hymn, reading one or two of the Psalms or Canticles, a passage of Scripture, catechism, or spiritual reading for meditation, and chanting our Lady's Magnificat, praying for various intentions, and/or dedicating the day to Our Lord. But families can adapt this format to the times and seasons of their lives. If your day begins to fray, take time to pray.

The Canticle of Zechariah: Luke 1

Blessed be the Lord God of Israel;
because He hath visited and wrought the redemption of
His people:
And hath raised up an horn of salvation to us,
in the house of David His servant:
As He spoke by the mouth of His holy prophets,
who are from the beginning:
Salvation from our enemies,
and from the hand of all that hate us:
To perform mercy to our fathers,

and to remember His holy testament,
the oath, which He swore to Abraham our father,
that He would grant to us,
that being delivered from the hand of our enemies,
we may serve Him without fear,
in holiness and justice before Him, all our days.
And thou, child, shalt be called the prophet of the Highest:
for thou shalt go before the face of the Lord to prepare
His ways:
To give knowledge of salvation to His people,
unto the remission of their sins:
Through the bowels of the mercy of our God,
in which the Orient from on high hath visited us:
To enlighten them that sit in darkness,
and in the shadow of death:
to direct our feet into the way of peace.

Evening Prayer

This is a little more difficult for families to pray, as it often overlaps with night prayer, but it can be prayed at dinnertime, or when the family gathers together at the end of a long day outside the home. At the recommendation of St. Louis de Montfort, I have also used this as a thanksgiving after receiving Jesus in Holy Communion.

The Canticle of Mary: Luke 2
My soul doth magnify the Lord, and my spirit hath
rejoiced in God my Savior. Because He hath regarded the
humility of His handmaid; for behold from henceforth all

generations shall call me blessed.
Because He that is mighty hath done great things to me;
and holy is His name.
And His mercy is from generation unto generations,
to them that fear Him.
He hath showed might in His arm:
He hath scattered the proud in the conceit of their heart.
He hath put down the mighty from their seat,
and hath exalted the humble.
He hath filled the hungry with good things;
and the rich He hath sent empty away.
He hath received Israel His servant,
being mindful of His mercy:
As He spoke to our fathers,
to Abraham and to His seed forever.

Night Prayer

The Liturgy of the Hours is the prayer of the Church, the one hundred and fifty Psalms chanted daily, morning, noon, and night. Night prayer has the fewest variations and can be memorized. This may be one of the easiest times for families to pray, particularly with older children. The father prays the antiphons and the first verse of each prayer, then the rest of the family responds with the next verse, and so on. When the children are older, we have the sons pray along with the father while the mother leads the daughters in the alternating verses. Our family often prays night prayer before the evening's entertainment, such as watching a favorite movie or show. Saturday night prayer is particularly lovely: after a long and weary day, it is a sweet balm to the soul. Night prayer begins with an examination of conscience and a chance for family members to ask forgiveness of one another. The father apologizing to his wife or children for any faults he has committed can set a humble example. Then the Confiteor (p. 76) is prayed to beg God's forgiveness for all our venial sins, and prayer ends with the Canticle of Simeon.

The Canticle of Simeon

Now Thou dost dismiss Thy servant, O Lord,
according to Thy word in peace;
because my eyes have seen Thy salvation,
Which Thou has prepared before the face of all peoples: A light of revelation to the Gentiles,
and the glory of Thy people Israel.

 # The Angelus

One of the hallmarks of lay Catholic life is the Angelus, prayed at six in the morning, noon, and six in the evening (we usually pray it before dinner). If you have a dinner bell in the house, it can be rung — something a toddler loves to do—and the family can pause in the work and pray together. It works well as a blessing before lunch and can be a reminder to the workaholics to pause to eat lunch as well as pray! When non-Catholic Christians are present, you can point out the Scriptures which constitute the prayer, and pray the final prayer slowly so they can follow its message:

L: The Angel of the Lord declared unto Mary
R: and she conceived by the Holy Spirit.
Hail Mary…

L: Behold the handmaid of the Lord!
R: Be it done unto me according to Thy Word.
Hail Mary….

(All genuflect)
L: And the Word was made flesh
R: and dwelt among us.
Hail Mary…

L: Pray for us, O Holy Mother of God
R: that we may be made worthy of the promises of Christ.

L: Let us pray:
Pour forth, we beseech Thee, O Lord, Thy Grace into our hearts, that we, to whom the Incarnation of Christ, Thy Son, was made known by the message of an angel, may by His Passion and Cross be brought to the glory of His Resurrection, Through the same Christ Our Lord. Amen.

A prayer of Spiritual Adoption
for an unborn child in danger of abortion
First composed by pro-life warrior Venerable Fulton Sheen, our family prays this directly after the Angelus: it is a constant reminder of the scourge of abortion and the small part we can do every day to mitigate it:
Jesus, Mary, and Joseph, we love You very much. We beg You to spare the life of the unborn child whom we have spiritually adopted who is in danger of abortion.
Amen.

The Regina Caeli

This is prayed at Easter season instead of the Angelus. It may be prayed formally or sung in Latin. We have included the version we use with our youngest children, which only requires the vigorous response "Alleluia!" (usually prayed in increasingly resounding Easter shouts.)

L: O Queen of Heaven, rejoice!
R: Alleluia!

L: For the Son Whom you merited to bear…
R: Alleluia!

L: has risen as He said!
R: Alleluia!

L: Pray for us to God.
R: Alleluia!

L: Rejoice, and be glad, O Virgin Mary!
R: Alleluia!

L: For the LORD is truly risen!
R: Alleluia!

L: Let us pray:
O God, Who gave joy to the whole world through the resurrection of Your Son, our Lord Jesus Christ, grant we beseech Thee, that through the intercession of the Virgin Mary, His Mother, we may obtain the joys of everlasting life. Through the same Christ our Lord.

R: Amen, alleluia!

V. Regina caeli, laetare, alleluia.
R. Quia quem meruisti portare, alleluia.

V. Resurrexit, sicut dixit, alleluia.
R. Ora pro nobis Deum, alleluia.

V. Gaude et laetare, Virgo Maria, alleluia.
R. Quia surrexit Dominus vere, alleluia.

Oremus. Deus, qui per resurrectionem Filii tui, Domini nostri Iesu Christi, mundum laetificare dignatus es: praesta, quaesumus; ut per eius Genetricem Virginem Mariam, perpetuae capiamus gaudia vitae. Per eundem Christum Dominum nostrum. **Amen.**

The Divine Mercy Chaplet

Modern times have seen the recovery of the Hour of Mercy, the three o'clock hour in which Christ died on the cross for our sins (Matthew 27:45-50), and when Peter and John went to the temple to pray (Acts 3:1), possibly to commemorate the same hour. Three o'clock can be a difficult hour to stay awake: children may be napping, and the body feels the weariness of the day's work. Pausing to bring to mind the sacrifice of Christ with the Divine Mercy prayer or praying a Divine Mercy chaplet, a brief devotion prayed on rosary beads, is an opportunity for a break from work. Children can easily learn the chaplet, and non-Catholic Christians can find the prayers very moving.

Similar to the prayers of the Rosary, the chaplet prayers can be prayed in two parts: the leader praying the first part and others responding with the second part.

Begin with the Sign of the Cross.
Our Father … Hail Mary … I Believe…

On the large beads of the rosary, pray:
L: Eternal Father, I offer You the Body and Blood, Soul and Divinity of Your dearly beloved Son, Our Lord Jesus Christ,
R: in atonement for our sins and those of the whole world.

On the small beads pray:
L: For the sake of His sorrowful passion
R: have mercy on us and on the whole world.

At the end, pray three times:
L: Holy God, Holy Mighty One, Holy Immortal One
R: have mercy on us and on the whole world.

L: Let us pray:
Eternal God, in whom Mercy is endless and the treasury of compassion inexhaustible, look kindly upon us and increase Your mercy in us, that in difficult moments we might not despair nor become despondent, but with great confidence submit ourselves to Your Holy Will, which is Love and Mercy itself.
R: Amen.

 # The Family Rosary

The Rosary has a long history as a spiritual weapon, and it's a unique lay devotion, cultivated and nourished by the laity as a complement to the clergy's Liturgy of the Hours. The basic prayers of the rosary include the Our Father, Hail Mary, and Glory Be, with the addition of the Apostle's Creed beforehand and ending with the Salve Regina, or Hail Holy Queen. Father Peyton, the "Rosary Priest" who promoted the family rosary, would say, "The family that prays together stays together." I've made my own rhyme: "A Rosary a day keeps the devil away."

Coming home from college one evening I walked in on my family praying the rosary. That was a new experience for me. I fell in love with the rosary and have been praying it ever since.

A note on praying the Rosary with children: sometimes it is challenging for them to sit still during an entire rosary (although I commend parents who can achieve this with their kids!). I think my children have found it pleasant when we take walks together as a family while praying the Rosary. You could also allow them to do some other quiet activity, like drawing or coloring pictures of the mysteries of the rosary during the prayers. Other strategies may occur to you in the different seasons of life. In any case, I strongly encourage you to pray the daily Rosary with your family.

Begin the Rosary with the Sign of the Cross and pray the Apostle's Creed:

I believe in God, the Father Almighty, Creator of heaven and earth, and in Jesus Christ, His only Son, our Lord, Who was conceived by the Holy Spirit, born of the Virgin Mary, suffered under Pontius Pilate, was crucified, died, and was buried. He descended into Hell, the third day, He rose from the dead. He ascended into heaven, and is seated at the right hand of God the Father Almighty, from thence He shall come to judge the living and the dead.

R: I believe in the Holy Spirit, the Holy Catholic Church, the communion of saints, the forgiveness of sins, the resurrection of the body, and life everlasting. Amen.

Then pray: *Our Father... Hail Mary 3X...Glory Be*

For each of the five decades: *Our Father ... Hail Mary 10X ... Glory be (and Fatima Prayer)*

Fatima Prayer

In the apparitions at Fatima, the Blessed Mother requested an additional prayer to be prayed after each Glory be, which has become so habitual as to be automatic with many Catholics today.

O my Jesus, forgive us our sins, save us from the fires of Hell, lead all souls to heaven, especially those most in need of Thy mercy.

Hail, Holy Queen,

Mother of Mercy! Our life, our sweetness, and our hope! To thee do we cry, poor banished children of Eve, to thee do we send up our sighs, mourning and weeping in this valley of tears. Turn, then, most gracious advocate, thine eyes of mercy toward us; and after this our exile show unto us the blessed fruit of thy womb, Jesus;
O clement, O loving, O sweet virgin Mary!

L: Pray for us, O holy Mother of God
R: That we may be made worthy of the promises of Christ.

In Latin: (may be sung)

Salve, Regina, Mater misericordiae,

vita, dulcedo, et spes nostra, salve.
Ad te clamamus
exsules filii Evae,
ad te suspiramus, gementes et flentes
in hac lacrimarum valle.

Eia, ergo, advocata nostra, illos tuos
misericordes oculos ad nos converte;
et Iesum, benedictum fructum ventris tui,
nobis post hoc exsilium ostende.
O clemens, O pia, O dulcis Virgo Maria.

More post-Rosary prayers

After finishing the Rosary, some families may add on other prayers that are important to their family. Here we reproduce some of our family's usual prayers. Feel free to adapt or discover your own.

Prayer to the Queen of the Angels

August Queen of Heaven, sovereign Mistress of Angels, thou who from the beginning has received from God the power and mission to crush the head of Satan, we humbly beseech thee, to send thy holy legions, that under thy command and by thy power, they may pursue the evil spirits, encounter them on every side, resist their bold attacks, and drive them hence into the abyss of eternal woe. Amen.

Prayer to St. Michael

St. Michael the Archangel, defend us in battle. Be our protection against the wickedness and snares of the Devil. May God rebuke him, we humbly pray, and do thou, O Prince of the heavenly hosts, by the power of God, cast into hell Satan and all the evil spirits who prowl about the world seeking the ruin of souls. Amen.

Prayer to St. Joseph

St. Joseph, patron, protector, and provider of the Holy Family, please help us live in a spirit of poverty according to God's will, and please assist us in our struggles against the powers of darkness.

Family Prayer to the Sacred Heart of Jesus

Dear Sacred Heart of Jesus, we renew our pledge of love and loyalty to You. Please keep us always close to Your loving Heart and to the most pure Heart of Your Mother. May we love one another more and more each day, forgiving each other's faults as You forgive us our sins. Teach us how to see You in those we meet outside our home, and to love them as You love them with patience and charity. Please keep our love for You always strong by frequent Mass, Holy Communion, and Confession. Thank You, dear Jesus, King and Friend of our family, for all the blessings of this day. Protect us during this night: Help us all get to heaven as a family. Dear Sacred Heart of Jesus, protect our family. Amen.

7

the father as leader of liturgical prayer

Pray at all times in the Spirit, with all prayer and supplication. To that end keep alert with all perseverance, making supplication for all the saints.
Ephesians 6:18

The Catholic Church has enriched us with seasons and times for penance, for preparation, and for celebration. Mothers often bring the liturgical calendar into family life through special foods, special displays, and special activities. A father can communicate some of that richness through prayers appropriate to the cycle of liturgical seasons.

Some of the prayers found previously in this book can be used liturgically: for example, it's fitting to pray the Prayer to the Holy Spirit for nine days before Pentecost, the original novena; and Marian prayers can be offered up on Our Lady's feast days or during May. And of course, the Regina Caeli is prayed on Easter and all throughout the Easter season. Here is a general calendar that a father might want to consult for directing his family's seasonal prayers. Transition times (beginning of school, New Year, etc.) are good times for rededicating the family to prayer and adapting routines.

January: Feast of the Mother of God, Little Christmas, Baptism of our Lord

February: Candlemas, transition to Lent

March: Lent and Easter, St. Patrick, St. Joseph, Annunciation

April: Lent and Easter

May: Easter and Pentecost, Our Lady

June: Sacred Heart of Jesus & Immaculate Heart of Mary

July: Precious Blood of Jesus

August: Assumption and Queenship of Mary

September: Our Lady of Sorrows, transition

October: The Holy Rosary

November: All Saints, Souls in Purgatory, Christ the King

December: Advent and Christmas

Advent Prayers

Blessing of the Advent Wreath

L: Our help is in the name of the Lord.

R: Who made heaven and earth.

L: O God, by whose Word all things are sanctified, pour forth Your blessing upon this wreath and grant that we who use it may prepare our hearts for the coming of Christ and may receive from You abundant graces. We ask this through Christ our Lord.

R: Amen.

The wreath may be sprinkled with holy water. The following prayers can be prayed for each of the four weeks of the season while the appropriate candle on the wreath is lit:

Week 1:

L: O Lord, stir up Thy might, we beg Thee, and come, that by Thy protection we may deserve to be rescued from the threatening dangers of our sins and saved by Thy deliverance. Through Christ our Lord. Amen.

Week 2:

L: O Lord, stir up our hearts that we may prepare for Thy only begotten Son, that through His coming we may be made worthy to serve Thee with pure minds. Through Christ our Lord. Amen.

Week 3:

L: O Lord, we beg Thee, incline Thy ear to our prayers and enlighten the darkness of our minds by the grace of Thy visitation. Through Christ our Lord. Amen.

Week 4

L: O Lord, stir up Thy power, we pray Thee, and come; and with great might help us, that with the help of Thy Grace, Thy merciful forgiveness may hasten what our sins impede. Through Christ our Lord. Amen.

St. Andrew's Christmas Novena

This Advent novena is traditionally prayed for a particular intention beginning on the feast of St. Andrew the Apostle (November 30) every day until Christmas day. We usually pray it after the Angelus or along with grace before meals throughout Advent and ending on Christmas day. Throughout the Christmas season, we continue to pray it by changing the line to: "In that hour I thank Thee, my God, for hearing my prayers and granting my desires..." to thank Him for His answered prayers.

Hail and blessed be the hour and moment when the Son of God was born of the most pure Virgin Mary at midnight in Bethlehem in the piercing cold. In that hour, vouchsafe, O Thou my God, to hear my prayers and grant my desires through Jesus Christ and His Blessed Mother and St. Joseph. Amen.

St. Andrew the Apostle, pray for us.

The Christmas Novena

This meditation on the journey of Mary and Joseph to Bethlehem is prayed the evening of the nine days before Christmas, beginning December 16 and ending on Christmas Eve. Consider singing the consecutive verses of "O Come Emmanuel" after praying each night's prayer. After each meditation pray this prayer:

Let us offer our hearts to the Holy Pilgrims as a dwelling where they may rest as we pray: **Jesus, Mary and Joseph, I give you my heart and my soul.**

Dec 16: Rebuking Covetousness. Consider the humility, and the poverty, with which our most pure Queen began the journey. She took nothing but the most necessary food and traveled over the snow-covered mountains. Consider how the Divine Child, within His virginal tabernacle, saw in His mind's eye, the very few who would follow the difficult and painful journey of the Way of the Cross, to reach the eternal resting place of His glory, and the many who would be lost on the broad way that leads to destruction. Ask yourself if you are following the Way that leads to the high mount of Eternal Joys. Pray fervently to the Holy Pilgrims, St. Joseph and the Blessed Virgin Mary, with the Holy Child Jesus still hidden in her womb for a generous heart, that they may admit you into their company, so that you may safely reach the heavenly Bethlehem.

Dec 17: Rebuking Gluttony. O most pure Mary, chosen from eternity by the decree of the Most High to be Mother of the Divine Word, you are full of all grace and virtues. You always acted with prudence and were obedient, not only to the laws of the Most High, but to the command of an earthly ruler. As soon as the edict of Caesar is published, without putting forth any opposition, you went forth in company with your holy Spouse from Nazareth to the great City of David, to register your names for the Roman census. Neither your great poverty, nor the length and perils of the journey make you seek an exemption or ask for an easier way. Teach me to be restrained and prudent as you were.

Dec 18. Rebuking Wrath. How often have I reacted in anger when I experience trials and suffering? Refusing to forgive, holding onto wrongs, thus depriving my soul of the presence of God, and making of it a dwelling for the evil spirit through sin? My soul, open today the doors of my heart, and hear the voice of Him who calls to us from the womb of His Mother: Behold, I stand at the gate and knock. Open to Me, for I have no place to lay My head. I come to let you share in My glory.

Dec 19: Rebuking Envy. Consider the troubles and the sufferings our Blessed Lady experienced, from the rain and cold on this journey. Consider how St. Joseph, worn out by the long journey on foot, goes from door to door, anxiously asking for a place wherein his Beloved Spouse might find rest. He receives only hard words and harsh refusals and no kindness towards them. As Mary and

Joseph perceive that all the doors of this city are closed against the Light of God Himself, their sorrow is increased. O Blessed Virgin, teach me kindness and let me not compare myself to others.

Dec 20: Rebuking Sloth. O my Blessed Lady and Mother, never will I cease to bless the Lord for your zeal for the Most High, and for all the heroic virtues and graces with which He was pleased to enrich you. I will forever admire the bountiful hand that gave you such privileges. And by your gift of singular diligence in following the Most High, I pray that you may obtain for me from your Divine Son the grace to practice this virtue, and all other virtues that I need for my sanctification to the end, that I may be worthy to enjoy God eternally. Amen.

Dec 21: Rebuking Lust. O Most pure Blessed Mother and good St. Joseph, the hardships you endured must have been painful. And yet, O most afflicted Mother, you directed your efforts to consoling your distressed Spouse with pleasant and holy conversation, keeping from him with blessed and holy prudence what was taking place in your own soul. And on reaching a place of rest, you joyfully reclined in the shelter of a lowly cave as if it was the place best befitting your dignity. And St. Joseph, you never once faltered in your charge to guard and protect the Child Within and His Mother. Thus you give us an example of the love and purity of heart we ought to practice in our trials and difficulties.

Dec 22: Rebuking Pride. O my soul, how far from God I am, even when I do what is right, if I do it for my own glory, and not for the love of our Savior Jesus. Consider how often you yourself show utter disregard in your heart for the Divine Child and even cast Him out, so as to do your own will and pleasure in pride. During this journey, go out to meet the Infant as the lepers did, and pray that He might cleanse you; for He comes to earth in order that He may cleanse the human race from the leprosy of sin.

Dec 23: Consider the feelings of holy Joseph as he went through the streets of Bethlehem in search of some kind of shelter for his holy spouse, the Queen of Heaven and earth. Every one, at the sight of his poverty and humility, looked upon him as a lazy vagabond. Contemplate the sorrow that must have come upon the Divine Child at the thought of His Mother's pitiable condition, and at the knowledge of man's willful deafness and hardness of heart towards Him. My soul, open wide your portals to receive the most Holy Virgin and your Infant God! Go out to meet Him and welcome Him with warm affection when He comes to you in Holy Communion. Keep Him always within your shelter, so that at the end of your journey here on earth, He in turn will welcome you into everlasting glory.

Dec 24: O Sovereign Lord, Infinite and Incomprehensible God, in the name of all creatures I give You thanks for coming into this world. You came to deliver us from the slavery and power of the evil spirit, and to make peace between man and his Creator. I welcome You with the greatest joy, for in Your love, You have come to open to us the way to our Father's House, where we might enjoy the glory of Your Divine Beauty. Welcome, my sweet Jesus, a thousand times welcome!

Dec 25: O God of Mercy, may You be blessed a thousand times for coming into the world as a tiny Child. This coming of Yours puts our pride and vanity to shame and teaches us true humility. This coming redeems us from the pride, lust, greed, gluttony, envy, anger, and sloth to which we were enslaved. I adore you, Christ Jesus, true God and true Man, and in token of my lasting appreciation, I offer you my heart filled with deepest love and humble gratitude.

Epiphany House Blessing

For this blessing, traditionally done on the Feast of Epiphany, holy water and chalk are needed, and a copy of the Gospel of Matthew for the reading. This ceremony can be simple or elaborate: children often like to process around the house after the father, carrying statues of the three kings from the family nativity scene, and singing "We Three Kings." But pageantry aside, this is a time-honored and worthy tradition.

Blessing the Chalk

L: The Lord shall watch over your going out and your coming in:

R: From this time forth forevermore.

L: Let us pray.

Loving God, bless this chalk which You have created, that it may be helpful to Your people; and grant that through the invocation of Your most Holy Name all who use it in faith to write upon the doors of their homes the names of Your saints, Caspar, Melchior, and Balthazar, may receive health of body and protection of soul for all who dwell in or visit their home; through Jesus Christ our Lord. R: Amen.

Sprinkle the chalk with holy water. Now is the procession. The father walks from room to room, sprinkling holy water as he goes to various entrance doors, with the family members following after him. Using the blessed chalk, the father marks the lintel of each entrance as follows:
20 + C + M + B + (YEAR)

L: The three Wise Men, Caspar, Melchior, and Balthazar followed the star of God's Son Who became man over two thousand years ago. May Christ bless our home and remain with us throughout the new year.
R: Amen.

L: Visit, O blessed Lord, this home with the gladness of Your presence. Bless all who live or visit here with the gift of Your love; and grant that we may manifest Your love to each other and to all whose lives we touch. May we grow in grace and in the knowledge and love of You; guide, comfort, and strengthen us in peace, O Jesus Christ, now and forever.
R: Amen.

Baptism of the Lord: Renewal of Promises

It is fitting to renew our baptismal promises on this feast day which ends Christmas in the New Rite. But this renewal is edifying for other occasions as well, such as a family member's birthday or baptismal day, or for anyone who wants to resolve to turn away from serious sin.

L. Do you reject Satan?

R. I do.

L. And all his works?

R. I do.

L. And all his empty promises?

R. I do.

L. Do you believe in God, the Father Almighty, creator of heaven and earth?

R. I do.

L. Do you believe in Jesus Christ, His only Son, our Lord, Who was born of the Virgin Mary was crucified, died, and was buried, rose from the dead, and is now seated at the right hand of the Father?

R. I do.

L. Do you believe in the Holy Spirit, the holy Catholic Church, the communion of saints, the forgiveness of sins, the resurrection of the body, and life everlasting?

R. I do.

L. God, the all-powerful Father of our Lord Jesus Christ has given us a new birth by water and the Holy Spirit and forgiven all our sins. May He also keep us faithful to our Lord Jesus Christ for ever and ever.

R. Amen.

The Feast of Candlemas

Candlemas, the feast of the Presentation of Jesus in the Temple on February 2, ends the Christmas season in the Old Rite. Given that blessed candles are important to have in a Catholic home, this feast is a good time to ensure that at least two are in the home.

LORD Jesus Christ, You are the true Light enlightening every soul born into this world. Today we celebrate the feast of Candlemas. Before Holy Mass, the priest blesses the candles, whose wax is the humming summer's work of countless bees. The flames of these candles will shed their light upon the altar at the Holy Sacrifice. Help us to realize, this day and every day, that our own humdrum daily work, if it is done for love of You, and in union with the Holy Sacrifice of the Mass, will be a supernatural work, and will shine brightly before You for all eternity. Help us realize, too, each time we see the blessed candles at Holy Mass, or at the bedside of the sick, that they are a symbol of Yourself, the Light shining in the darkness of this world. Help us to live in that Light, to make it our own, and to kindle it in the souls of others, increasing the area of light and lessening the darkness in the World. This, dear Lord, help us do, through the merits of Your own dear mother, Mary, who did everything for love of You, from the moment she brought You into this world till the day she joined You in the realms of light at the end of her earthly life. Then we, too, working for You, shall be light-bearers who will help to spread Your kingdom on earth, and increase the number of those who dwell in heaven, the city of eternal light. Amen.

Feast of St. Patrick: St. Patrick's Breastplate

Here is a short version of an appropriate St. Patrick's Day prayer composed by the saint himself.

Christ be with me, Christ within me

Christ behind me, Christ before me

Christ beside me, Christ to win me

Christ to comfort me and restore me.

Christ beneath me, Christ above me

Christ in quiet, Christ in danger

Christ in hearts of all that love me

Christ in mouth of friend or stranger.

Sorrows and Joys of St. Joseph

These prayers are especially appropriate to pray on the Feast of St. Joseph, Husband of Mary, March 19. An Our Father, Hail Mary, and Glory Be can be prayed after each section.

1. ST. JOSEPH, Chaste Spouse of the Holy Mother of God, by the SORROW with which thy heart was pierced at the thought of a cruel separation from Mary, and by the deep JOY that thou didst feel when the angel revealed to thee the ineffable mystery of the Incarnation, obtain for us from Jesus and Mary, the grace of surmounting all anxiety. Win for us from the Adorable Heart of Jesus the unspeakable peace of which He is the Eternal Source.

2. ST. JOSEPH, Foster-Father of Jesus, by the bitter SORROW which thy heart experienced in seeing the Child Jesus lying in a manger, and by the JOY which thou

didst feel in seeing the Wise men recognize and adore Him as their God, obtain by thy prayers that our heart, purified by thy protection, may become a living crib, where the Savior of the world may receive and bless our homage.

3. ST. JOSEPH, by the SORROW with which thy heart was pierced at the sight of the Blood which flowed from the Infant Jesus in the Circumcision, and by the JOY that inundated thy soul at thy privilege of imposing the sacred and mysterious Name of Jesus, obtain for us that the merits of this Precious Blood may be applied to our souls, and that the Divine Name of Jesus may be engraved forever in our hearts.

4. ST. JOSEPH, by thy SORROW when Simeon prophesied that the soul of Mary would be pierced with a sword of sorrow, and by thy JOY when holy Simeon added that the Divine Infant was to be the resurrection of many, obtain for us the grace to have compassion on the sorrows of Mary, and share in the salvation which Jesus brought to the earth.

5. ST. JOSEPH, by thy SORROW when told to fly into Egypt, and by thy JOY in seeing the idols overthrown at the arrival of the living God, grant that no idol of earthly affection may any longer occupy our hearts, but being like thee entirely devoted to the service of Jesus and Mary, we may live and happily die for them alone.

6. ST. JOSEPH, by the SORROW of thy heart caused by the fear of the tyrant Archelaus and by the JOY in sharing the company of Jesus and Mary at Nazareth, obtain for us, that disengaged from all fear, we may enjoy the peace of a good conscience and may live in security, in union with Jesus and Mary, experiencing the effect of thy salutary assistance at the hour of our death.

7. ST. JOSEPH, by the bitter SORROW with which the loss of the Child Jesus crushed thy heart, and by the holy JOY which inundated thy soul in recovering thy Treasure on entering the Temple, we supplicate thee not to permit us to lose our Savior Jesus by sin. Yet should this misfortune befall us, grant that we may share thy eagerness in seeking Him, and obtain for us the grace to find Him again, ready to show us His great mercy, especially at the hour of death; so that we may pass from this life to enjoy His presence in heaven, there to sing with thee His divine mercies forever.

Let us pray: O God, Who in Thine ineffable Providence has vouchsafed to choose Blessed Joseph to be the Spouse of Thy most holy Mother; grant, we beseech Thee, that we may deserve to have him for our intercessor in heaven whom on earth we venerate as our holy protector. Through Christ our Lord. Amen.

Lenten and Easter Prayers

Lent is the time when we, personally and as a family, make sacrifices. Some of these may be private, but I've found it helpful to consult with my wife about my penances and then hold a family meeting to discuss our Lenten practices. That way we can hold one another accountable and join together in doing apostolic work for the poor, or giving up treats or movies, or engaging in extra prayers or devotions such as the Stations of the Cross on Fridays.

As Lent gets close to the Triduum, you may want to revisit your family Lenten practices and perhaps add a little more. The Church has beautiful liturgical feasts during Holy Thursday, Good Friday, and the Easter Vigil that the entire family can participate in. Enabling the family to worship together at these services is often part of the domestic priest's responsibilities, whether that means holding the baby during a long service or making an extra trip to pick up a teenager from work in order to make a Good Friday service.

We begin the Divine Mercy Novena on Good Friday and continue it for the next nine days until Divine Mercy Sunday. And on Easter morning, we change from the Angelus to the "Alleluia!" of the Regina Caeli (p. 91), setting the joyful tone for the season.

A Very Short Way of the Cross

This was created by the Franciscan Fathers on their missions but works well for parents with small children. Before each station say:
L: We adore You, O Christ, and we praise You…

R: Because by Your holy Cross, You have redeemed the world.

After each station, you can pause and if desired, pray an Our Father, Hail Mary, and Glory Be.

First Station: Jesus is condemned to death.
O Jesus! so meek and uncomplaining, teach me resignation in trials.

Second Station: Jesus accepts His Cross.
My Jesus, this Cross should be mine, not Thine; my sins crucified Thee.

Third Station: Jesus falls the first time.
O Jesus! by this first fall, never let me fall into mortal sin.

Fourth Station: Jesus meets His Mother.
O Jesus! may no human tie, however dear, keep me from following the road of the Cross.

Fifth Station: Simon helps Jesus carry His Cross.
Simon unwillingly assisted Thee; may I suffer all with patience for Thee.

Sixth Station: Veronica wipes the face of Jesus.
O Jesus! Thou didst imprint Thy sacred features upon Veronica's veil; stamp them also indelibly upon my heart.

Seventh Station: Jesus falls the second time.
By Thy second fall, preserve me, dear Lord, from relapse into sin.

Eighth Station: Jesus consoles the women of Jerusalem.
My greatest consolation would be to hear Thee say: "Your sins are forgiven thee, because thou hast loved much."

Ninth Station: Jesus falls the third time.
O Jesus! When I am weary upon life's long journey, be Thou my strength and my perseverance.

Tenth Station: Jesus is stripped of His garments.
My soul has been robbed of its robe of innocence; clothe me, dear Jesus, with the garb of penance and contrition.

Eleventh Station: Jesus is nailed to the Cross.
Thou didst forgive Thy enemies; my God, teach me to forgive injuries and FORGET them.

Twelfth Station: Jesus dies on the Cross.
Thou art dying, my Jesus, but Thy Sacred Heart still throbs with love for Thy sinful children.

Thirteenth Station: Jesus is taken down from the Cross.
Receive me into thy arms, O Sorrowful Mother; and obtain for me perfect contrition for my sins.

Fourteenth Station: Jesus is laid in the tomb.
When I receive Thee into my heart in Holy Communion, O Jesus, make it a fit abiding place for Thy adorable Body. Amen.

Holy Thursday: Visit to the Blessed Sacrament

After the long evening Mass on Holy Thursday, we are invited to watch one hour with Jesus in Eucharistic adoration. I would frequently arrange to do this with my older children while my wife stayed home with the small children. This prayer is based on prayers composed by St. Alphonsus Liguori.

My LORD Jesus Christ, Who because of Your love for men remain night and day in the Blessed Sacrament, full of pity and of love, awaiting, calling and welcoming all who come to visit You, I believe that You are present here on the altar. I adore You, and I thank You for all the graces You have bestowed on me, especially for having given me Yourself in this Sacrament, for having given me Your most holy Mother Mary to plead for me, and for having called me to visit You in this church. I now salute Your most loving Heart, and that for three ends: first, in thanksgiving for this great gift; second, to make amends to You for all the outrages committed against You in this Sacrament by Your enemies; third, I intend by this visit to adore You in all the places on earth in which You are present in the Blessed Sacrament and in which You are least honored and most abandoned.

My Jesus, I love You with my whole heart. I am very sorry for having so many times offended Your infinite goodness. With the help of Your grace, I purpose never to offend You again. And now, unworthy though I am, I consecrate myself to You without reserve. I renounce and give entirely to You my will, my affection, my desires and all that I possess. For the future, dispose of me and all I have as You please. All I ask of You is Your holy love, final perseverance and that I may carry out Your will perfectly.

I recommend to You the souls in Purgatory, especially those who had the greatest devotion to the Blessed Sacrament and to the Blessed Virgin Mary. I also recommend to You all poor sinners.

Finally, my dear Savior, I unite all my desires with the desires of Your most loving Heart; and I offer them, thus united, to the Eternal Father, and beseech Him, in Your name and for love of You, to accept and grant them.

The Divine Mercy Novena

This novena begins on Good Friday and is prayed daily until the Feast of Divine Mercy on the Sunday after Easter. Begin each day's prayers with the Chaplet of Divine Mercy (p. 92) and then read the intention asked for by Our Lord and the prayer for each day.

First Day: *"Today bring to Me all mankind, especially all sinners, and immerse them in the ocean of My mercy. In this way you will console Me in the bitter grief into which the loss of souls plunges Me."*

Most Merciful Jesus, whose very nature it is to have compassion on us and to forgive us, do not look upon our sins but upon our trust which we place in Your infinite goodness. Receive us all into the abode of Your Most Compassionate Heart, and never let us escape from It. We beg this of You by Your love which unites You to the Father and the Holy Spirit.

Eternal Father, turn Your merciful gaze upon all mankind and especially upon poor sinners, all enfolded in the Most Compassionate Heart of Jesus. For the sake of His sorrowful Passion show us Your mercy, that we may praise the omnipotence of Your mercy for ever and ever. Amen.

Second Day: *"Today bring to Me the souls of priests and religious and immerse them in My unfathomable mercy. It was they who gave Me strength to endure My bitter Passion. Through them as through channels My mercy flows out upon mankind."*

Most Merciful Jesus, from whom comes all that is good, increase Your grace in men and women consecrated to Your service, that they may perform worthy works of mercy; and that all who see them may glorify the Father of Mercy who is in heaven.

Eternal Father, turn Your merciful gaze upon the company of chosen ones in Your vineyard—upon the souls of priests and religious; and endow them with the strength of Your blessing. For the love of the Heart of Your Son in which they are enfolded, impart to them Your power and light, that they may be able to guide others in the way of salvation and with one voice sing praise to Your boundless mercy for ages without end. Amen.

Third Day: *"Today bring to Me all devout and faithful souls, and immerse them in the ocean of My mercy. These souls brought Me consolation on the Way of the Cross. They were that drop of consolation in the midst of an ocean of bitterness."*

Most Merciful Jesus, from the treasury of Your mercy, You impart Your graces in great abundance to each and all. Receive us into the abode of Your Most Compassionate Heart and never let us escape from It. We beg this grace of You by that most wonderous love for the heavenly Father with which Your Heart burns so fiercely.

Eternal Father, turn Your merciful gaze upon faithful souls, as upon the inheritance of Your Son. For the sake of His sorrowful Passion, grant them Your blessing and surround them with Your constant protection. Thus may they never fail in love or lose the treasure of the holy faith, but rather, with all the hosts of Angels and Saints, may they glorify Your boundless mercy for endless ages. Amen.

Fourth Day: *"Today bring to Me the pagans and those who do not yet know Me. I was thinking also of them during My bitter Passion, and their future zeal comforted My Heart. Immerse them in the ocean of My mercy."*

Most compassionate Jesus, You are the Light of the whole world. Receive into the abode of Your Most Compassionate Heart the souls of those who do not believe in God and of those who as yet do not know You. Let the rays of Your grace enlighten them that they, too, together with us, may extol Your wonderful mercy; and do not let them escape from the abode which is Your Most Compassionate Heart.

Eternal Father, turn Your merciful gaze upon the souls of those who do not believe in You, and of those who as yet do not know You, but who are enclosed in the Most Compassionate Heart of Jesus. Draw them to the light of the Gospel. These souls do not know what great happiness it is to love You. Grant that they, too, may extol the generosity of Your mercy for endless ages. Amen.

Fifth Day: *"Today bring to Me the souls of those who have separated themselves from My Church and immerse them in the ocean of My mercy. During My bitter Passion they tore at My Body and Heart, that is, My Church. As they return to unity with the Church, My wounds heal and in this way they alleviate My Passion."*

Most Merciful Jesus, Goodness Itself, You do not refuse light to those who seek it of You. Receive into the abode of Your Most Compassionate Heart the souls of those who have separated themselves from Your Church. Draw them by Your light into the unity of the Church, and do not let them escape from the abode of Your Most Compassionate Heart; but bring it about that they, too, come to glorify the generosity of Your mercy.

Eternal Father, turn Your merciful gaze upon the souls of those who have separated themselves from Your Son's Church, who have squandered Your blessings and misused Your graces by obstinately persisting in their errors. Do not look upon their errors, but upon the love of Your own Son and upon His bitter Passion, which He underwent for their sake, since they, too, are enclosed in His Most Compassionate Heart. Bring it about that they also may glorify Your great mercy for endless ages. Amen.

Sixth Day: *"Today bring to Me the meek and humble souls and the souls of little children, and immerse them in My mercy. These souls most closely resemble My Heart. They strengthened Me during My bitter agony. I saw them as earthly Angels, who will keep vigil at My altars. I pour out upon them whole torrents of grace. Only the humble soul is capable of receiving My grace. I favor humble souls with My confidence."*

Most Merciful Jesus, You yourself have said, "Learn from Me for I am meek and humble of heart." Receive into the abode of Your Most Compassionate Heart all meek and humble souls and the souls of little children. These souls send all heaven into ecstasy and they are the heavenly Father's favorites. They are a sweet-smelling bouquet before the throne of God; God Himself takes delight in their fragrance. These souls have a permanent abode in Your Most Compassionate Heart, O Jesus, and they unceasingly sing out a hymn of love and mercy.

Eternal Father, turn Your merciful gaze upon meek souls, upon humble souls, and upon little children who are enfolded in the abode which is the Most Compassionate Heart of Jesus. These souls bear the closest resemblance to Your Son. Their fragrance rises from the earth and reaches Your very throne. Father of mercy and of all goodness, I beg You by the love You bear these souls and by the delight You take in them: Bless the whole world, that all souls together may sing out the praises of Your mercy for endless ages. Amen.

Seventh Day: *"Today bring to Me the souls who especially venerate and glorify My mercy and immerse them in My mercy. These souls sorrowed most over my Passion and entered most deeply into My spirit. They are living images of My Compassionate Heart. These souls will shine with a special brightness in the next life. Not one of them will go into the fire of hell. I shall particularly defend each one of them at the hour of death."*

Most Merciful Jesus, whose Heart is Love Itself, receive into the abode of Your Most Compassionate Heart the souls of those who particularly extol and venerate the greatness of Your mercy. These souls are mighty with the very power of God Himself. In the midst of all afflictions and adversities they go forward, confident of Your mercy; and united to You, O Jesus, they carry all mankind on their shoulders. These souls will not be judged severely, but Your mercy will embrace them as they depart from this life.

Eternal Father, turn Your merciful gaze upon the souls who glorify and venerate Your greatest attribute, that of Your fathomless mercy, and who are enclosed in the Most Compassionate Heart of Jesus. These souls are a living Gospel; their hands are full of deeds of mercy, and their hearts, overflowing with joy, sing a canticle of mercy to You, O Most High! I beg You O God: Show them Your mercy according to the hope and trust they have placed in You. Let there be accomplished in them the promise of Jesus, who said to them that during their life, but especially at the hour of death, the souls who will venerate this fathomless mercy of His, He, Himself, will defend as His glory. Amen.

Eighth Day: *"Today bring to Me the souls who are detained in Purgatory and immerse them in the abyss of My mercy. Let the torrents of My Blood cool down their scorching flames. All these souls are greatly loved by Me. They are making retribution to My justice. It is in your power to bring them relief. Draw all the indulgences from the treasury of My Church and offer them on their behalf. Oh, if you only knew the torments they suffer, you would continually offer for them the alms of the spirit and pay off their debt to My justice."*

Most Merciful Jesus, You Yourself have said that You desire mercy; so I bring into the abode of Your Most Compassionate Heart the souls in Purgatory, souls who are very dear to You, and yet, who must make retribution to Your justice. May the streams of Blood and Water which gushed forth from Your Heart put out the flames of Purgatory, that there, too, the power of Your mercy may be celebrated.

Eternal Father, turn Your merciful gaze upon the souls suffering in Purgatory, who are enfolded in the Most Compassionate Heart of Jesus. I beg You, by the sorrowful Passion of Jesus Your Son, and by all the bitterness with which His most sacred Soul was flooded: Manifest Your mercy to the souls who are under Your just scrutiny. Look upon them in no other way but only through the Wounds of Jesus, Your dearly beloved Son; for we firmly believe that there is no limit to Your goodness and compassion. Amen.

Ninth Day: *"Today bring to Me souls who have become lukewarm and immerse them in the abyss of My mercy. These souls wound My Heart most painfully. My soul suffered the most dreadful loathing in the Garden of Olives because of lukewarm souls. They were the reason I cried out: 'Father, take this cup away from Me, if it be Your will.' For them, the last hope of salvation is to run to My mercy."*

Most compassionate Jesus, You are Compassion Itself. I bring lukewarm souls into the abode of Your Most Compassionate Heart. In this fire of Your pure love, let these tepid souls, who, like corpses, filled You with such deep loathing, be once again set aflame. O Most Compassionate Jesus, exercise the omnipotence of Your mercy and draw them into the very ardor of Your love, and bestow upon them the gift of holy love, for nothing is beyond Your power.

Eternal Father, turn Your merciful gaze upon lukewarm souls who are nonetheless enfolded in the Most Compassionate Heart of Jesus. Father of Mercy, I beg You by the bitter Passion of Your Son and by His three-hour agony on the Cross: Let them, too, glorify the abyss of Your mercy. Amen.

Pentecost Novena Prayer

The nine days between Ascension Thursday and Pentecost Sunday when Mary and the Apostles were praying for the coming of the Holy Spirit was the original novena. You can pray for a different fruit of the Holy Spirit on each day as enumerated in Galatians 5:22-23.

Opening prayer for all nine days:

Let us bow down in humility at the power and grandeur of the Holy Spirit. Let us worship the Holy Trinity and give glory today to the Paraclete, our Advocate.

O Holy Spirit, by Your power, Christ was raised from the dead to save us, and by Your grace, miracles are performed in Jesus' name. By Your love, we are protected from evil. And so, we ask with humility and a beggar's heart for Your gift of ______ within us.

Day 1: Charity

The great charity of all the host of Saints is only made possible by Your power, O Divine Spirit. Increase in us, the virtue of charity that we may love as God loves with the selflessness of the Saints.

Day 2: Joy

All of the Saints are marked with an uncompromisable joy in times of trial, difficulty and pain. Give us, O Holy Spirit, the joy that surpasses all understanding that we may live as a witness to Your love and fidelity!

Day 3: Peace

The Saints were tempted, attacked and accused by the devil who is the destroyer of peace. When we are accused by the devil, come to our aid as our Advocate and give us peace that lasts through all trials.

Day 4: Patience

O Holy Spirit, You give lavishly to those who ask. Please give us the patience of the Saints who are now with You in heaven. Help us to endure everything with an eternal patience that is only possible with Your help.

Day 5: Kindness

Jesus approached sinners with immense kindness. Holy Paraclete, please treat us humble sinners with the same kindness and give us the ability to treat all others with that kindness as well.

Day 6: Faithfulness

You, O Lord, are ever faithful. You are faithful until the end. Though we are weak and distracted, please give us the grace to be faithful to You as You are to us!

Day 7: Gentleness

Despite the gravity of our sins, O Lord, You treat us with gentleness. Dear Holy Spirit, give us Your power to treat all in our lives with the gentleness of the Saints.

Day 8: Self-Control

Your Martyrs had the overwhelming self-control to go joyfully to a painful death without shrinking from the opportunity to join You in heaven. Give us this self-control to have command over our emotions and desires that we may serve You more fully.

Day 9: Goodness

We want to be like your Saints in heaven. Holy Spirit, renew us by Your power with Your goodness that we may bring the Good News to the world.

Closing prayer each day: Come Holy Spirit (p. 75)

Prayer to the Trinity for Trinity Sunday

Glory be to the Father, Who by His almighty power and love created us, making us in the image and likeness of God. Glory be to the Son, Who by His Precious Blood delivered us from hell and opened for us the gates of heaven. Glory be to the Holy Spirit Who has sanctified us in the sacrament of Baptism and continues to sanctify us by the graces we receive daily from His bounty.

Glory be to the Three adorable Persons of the Holy Trinity, now and forever. Amen.

Fatima Prayer of Reparation

It seems appropriate to say this prayer on the Feast of Corpus Christi:
O Most Holy Trinity, Father, Son and Holy Spirit, I adore Thee profoundly. I offer Thee the most precious Body, Blood, Soul and Divinity of Jesus Christ present in all the tabernacles of the world, in reparation for the outrages, sacrileges and indifferences by which He is offended, and through the infinite merits of His Most Sacred Heart, the Immaculate Heart of Mary, (and the intercession of St. Joseph,) I beg the conversion of poor sinners. Amen.

Prayer to Christ the King

This may be prayed as a novena nine days before or simply on the Feast of Christ the King.
Almighty and merciful God, You break the power of evil and make all things new in your Son Jesus Christ, the King of the universe. May all in heaven and earth acclaim Your glory and never cease to praise You. O Lord our God, You alone are the Most Holy King and Ruler of all nations. We pray to You, Lord, in the great expectation of receiving from You, O Divine King, mercy, peace, justice and all good things. Protect, O Lord our King, our families and the land of our birth. Guard us, we pray, Most Faithful One. Protect us from our enemies and from Your just judgment. Forgive us, O Sovereign King, our sins against You. Jesus, You are the King of Mercy. We have deserved Your Just Judgment. Have mercy on us, Lord, and forgive us. We trust in Your Great Mercy. O most awe-inspiring

King, we bow before You and pray that Your reign, Your kingdom, be recognized on earth.
Amen.

L: Christ the King…
R: Your Kingdom come!

All: Long live Christ the King! Viva Cristo Rey!

We want God Who is our Father!
We want God Who is our King!

It seems fitting to end this prayer book with a prayer that echoes the reminder given to us in every Mass and last words of Scripture: Christ will come again. Come Lord Jesus! The father is there to remind his family most of all that this life, including our prayer, is but a preparation for the next life in Heaven.

Prayer for the Parousia

O Lord Jesus Christ, Thou said in the final words of Scripture, "Behold, I come quickly; and My reward is with Me, to render to every man according to his works. I am the Alpha and Omega, the first and the last, the beginning and the end."

Thou proclaimed: "Blessed are they that wash their robes in the blood of the Lamb: that they may have a right to the tree of life and may enter in by the gates into the city." Thou art the Root and Stock of David, the Bright and Morning Star. So we pray with the Spirit and the Bride: Come! And he that hears, let him say: Come! And he that thirsts, let him come: and he that will, let him take the water of life, freely.

R: O Lord, give us this water always!

L: We give Thee thanks, O Lord God Almighty, Who is, Who was, and Who is to come. Great and marvelous are Thy works, Lord God Almighty; just and true are all Thy ways, Thou King of saints. Praise our God, all ye His servants, and ye that fear Him, both small and great.

R: Amen! Even so, come Lord Jesus!

L: The grace of Our Lord Jesus Christ be with you all.

R: Amen.

Appendix A: a basic spiritual battle plan of life

Having gathered the following practices from saints and mentors older and wiser than I, I wrote this up for my sons and other young men as an example of a plan for a basic prayer life, but I've given it to my daughters as well with some modifications. It can be modified to fit your particular circumstances. It can also be used by those trying to leave old destructive behaviors and trying to establish new healthy holy habits. I'm including it here as a practical guide to begin implementing some of the prayers and practices outlined in this booklet. Amidst all your desires and demands on your time and attention, remember to...

"Seek first the kingdom of God and his righteousness, and all these things shall be yours as well." Matthew 6:33

Daily

Jesus says, *"Whoever wants to be My disciple must deny themselves and take up their cross <u>daily</u> and follow Me." (Luke 9:23)*

To begin, pick one thing from this list that you are not currently doing and start doing it.

Practice the Heroic moment

1. Get up at a fixed time each day, every day.
2. Make your bed as an act of penance out of love for Jesus. (If you are married, your wife will probably appreciate it too.)
3. Pray a morning offering, the morning Angelus, and/or three Hail Mary's for purity.

Take up a Spiritual Weapon

Scripture

The Word of God is sharper than any two-edged sword. (Hebrews 4:12) Read Scripture for at least a few minutes, then engage in quiet mental prayer thinking of what you've read. Feel free to tell God your thoughts on it. Then try to listen for His reply. If a passage of Scripture speaks to you, try committing it to memory.

Rosary

The rosary is the bible on beads. But you don't have to do it all at once. You can start with one decade and add more throughout the day. A rosary a day keeps the devil away.

Spiritual Armor (Ephesians 6:11-18)

Wear at least one of the following: a Brown scapular & miraculous medal, a crucifix & St. Benedict Medal.

Study the Catholic Faith

Know, love, and live your Catholic faith. To live it, you must love it. To love it, you must know it. To know it, you must study it.

Read one or more of the following for a few minutes daily.

- A Catholic Catechism. Besides the CCC, there is the classic *Baltimore Catechism*. I particularly recommend the *Roman Catechism* (of the Council of Trent).
- A good Catholic commentary on Scripture
- Spiritual reading. This can be writings of the saints, lives of the saints, or church history.

Small acts of mortification/self-denial.

Choose to do something that you're not inclined to do: take the initiative to wash the dishes, take out the garbage, sweep or vacuum a floor, clean a toilet, practice good posture, daily exercise, and just your daily duties done well. Offer these up for love of Jesus, the conversion of sinners, and in reparation for the sins committed against the Immaculate Heart of Mary.

Practice Purity

"Blessed are the pure of heart; they shall see God." (Matthew 5:8)

- Moderate your use of digital devices. Do you need an accountability partner?

- When you see a beautiful woman pray something like, "Thank you, Father, for the beauty of your daughters. Please give me grace to respect them."
- Ask St. Joseph to help you keep custody of your eyes.

Nightly Examination of Conscience

Examine your conscience briefly, asking Our Lord's pardon for any sins or faults, thank Him for His blessings, and pray an Act of Contrition before going to sleep.

Weekly

Implement one of the following practices weekly that you are not already doing.

Mass

In addition to Sundays & Holy Days of Obligation, try to attend at least one daily Mass per week as an act of love and thanks to God for all the good He has given you.

Larger act of self-denial once a week

Eg: fast one day a week, give up candy or cookies or coffee or soda, take a cold shower, exercise, or some other penance. Again, all for love of Jesus, conversion of sinners, and in reparation for sin.

Eucharistic Adoration

"Could you not watch one hour with Me? Watch and pray that you may not enter into temptation." (Matthew 26:40-41)

Try for one hour a week or maybe a few minutes on multiple days.

Monthly

Receive the Sacrament of Confession & Reconciliation. You might want to try for twice a month if needed.

Annually

Make a Spiritual Retreat to spend time alone with Our Lord. A weekend retreat is ideal, but a day retreat can work if you can't get away for long. Annual retreats are not a luxury: they're a necessity.

----

1 Corinthians 13:11-13

11 When I was a child, I talked like a child, I thought like a child, I reasoned like a child. **When I became a man**, I put the ways of childhood behind me.

12 For now we see only a reflection as in a mirror; then we shall see face to face. Now I know in part; then I shall know fully, even as I am fully known.

13 And now these three remain: faith, hope and love. But **the greatest of these is love.**

Some of the saints warn us not to overburden ourselves with devotions to the point where it interferes with the duties of our state in life but to endeavor to practice devotions, daily duties, and everything well for love of God. Love of God and neighbor is the heart of the law. On those two commandments hang all the law and the prophets, as Jesus said. (Mt 22:36-40)

If you feel over-challenged by all this, then just pick one or two things from the "Daily" section and work on doing them consistently. Once you have mastered that, you can work on becoming consistent about another exercise or devotion, and so on, building your battle victories and discipline. *Ask the Holy Spirit to guide you.* Check with a confessor or spiritual director. Remember: *"For the moment all discipline seems painful rather than pleasant; later it yields the peaceful fruit of righteousness to those who have been trained by it."* (Hebrews 12:11)

If you are a husband, another part of the spiritual battle to protect your wife is to take her on regular (at least monthly) dates. It doesn't have to be expensive, just an opportunity to spend leisure time together. Give her encouraging words, hugs and caresses, maybe even small gifts or notes of appreciation.

If you are a father, give regular time and attention to your children not only in prayer, but working with them, playing games with them, generally spending time with them, and giving them encouraging words and affection as well as guidance and gentle correction when needed.

Appendix B:
Liturgy for the Dedication of the Home as a Domestic Church

Priest/Deacon: Dear Members and Friends of this household:

It is an ancient and constant teaching of Holy Church that those who receive Baptism in the Church receive a priestly character which, though essentially different in kind from the character given in ordination to the sacramental priesthood, is nevertheless real and of deep significance.

It is also the teaching of the Church that the Catholic Christian family is intended by God to be such a nature as to deserve to be called a little Church; that all the baptized members of each family household are to exercise there, in appropriate ways, the priesthood conferred on them in baptism; and that the father is, by divine institution, appointed as chief pastor of this little Church, and his wife is appointed here, as elsewhere, to be his helpmeet, as Pope John XXIII taught in his encyclical, "Near the Chair of Peter" on June 29, 1959:

"Let the father of the family take the place of God among his children, and not only by his authority but by the upright example of his life also stand clearly in the first place. Let the mother, however, rule firmly over her offspring by gentleness and virtue in the domestic setting. Let her behave with indulgence and love towards her husband and, along with him, let her carefully instruct and train her family."

All this being so, dear friends, we are gathered together here today under the patronage of the Holy Virgin Mary, Mother of God and of the Church, and St. Joseph, head of the Holy Family and Patron of the Universal Church, to call down God's blessing on this household, to establish it as a little Church in which He may deign to dwell, and to install the father of the family as its pastor, and the mother as his divinely appointed assistant and loving counselor, so that it may become firmly established on the faith, and be the center of a widely radiating charity, grounded in a loving obedience to the Vicar of Christ and all bishops in union with him.

Blessing of the Home as a Domestic Church

Priest/Deacon: Peace to this house...

R: And to all who live in it.

Priest/Deacon: My house shall be called a house of prayer, says the Lord (Matt 21:13);

R: Like living stones let us be built on Christ as a spiritual house, a holy priesthood (1 Peter 2:5)

Priest/Deacon: You are the temple of God, and God's Spirit dwells in you. The temple of God is holy; you are that temple. (I Cor. 3:16)

R: Can it be indeed that God dwells among men on earth? Greatly to be feared is God in His sanctuary; He, the God of Israel, gives power and strength to His people. Blessed be God! (Ps. 68:35)

Priest/Deacon: Let us pray:
Look kindly on the prayer and petition of your servants, O Lord our God. May Your eyes watch night and day over this temple, where You have decreed You shall be honored. Listen to the petitions of Your servants which they offer in this earthly dwelling of Yours. Listen from Your heavenly dwelling and grant pardon and peace, to

the praise and glory of Your Name, for the good of our household and of all Your Church.

R: Amen.

Priest/Deacon: Unless the LORD build a house, they labor in vain who build it. (Psalm 127)

Blessed are all they that fear the Lord.
blessed are you and it shall be well with you;
Your wife shall be as a fruitful vine
on the walls of your house;
Your children as olive plants round about your table…

May the Lord bless you out of Zion
and may you see the good things of Jerusalem
all the days of your life;

May you see your children's children
and peace upon Israel. (Psalm 128)

Priest/Deacon: Let us pray:
Father, Who make Your Church on earth a sign of the new and eternal Jerusalem, send Your Holy Spirit upon this dwelling that it may become a temple of Your presence and a home of Your glory, through Jesus Christ, Your Son, our Lord, Who lives and reigns with You and the same Holy Spirit, one God, world without end.

R: Amen.

Installation of the Father & Mother as Pastor and Associate of the Domestic Church

Priest/Deacon: Whose household is this?

Husband and Wife: It is ours.

Priest/Deacon: Hear, Father of this house, appointed by God to rule with authority, and hear, Mother of this house, appointed by God to preside in love: The Lord is our God, the Lord alone! Therefore you shall love the Lord you God with all your heart, and with all your soul, and with all your strength. Take to heart these words with I enjoin on you today. Drill them into your children. Speak of them at home and abroad, whether you are busy or at rest. (Deut. 6:4-7)

Father: One thing I ask of the Lord, this I seek: to dwell in the house of the Lord all the days of my life.

Mother: That I may gaze on the loveliness of the Lord and contemplate His temple.

Father: Your presence, O Lord, I seek; hide not Your face from me;

Mother: I believe I shall see the bounty of the Lord in the land of the living.

All: Father, make them holy in the truth. As You sent Me into the world, I have sent them into the world. (John 17:17-18)

Priest/Deacon: I have found David my servant; with My holy oil I have anointed him, that My hand may be always with him, and that My arm may make him strong. (Ps. 89:20-21)

Let us pray: Father, accept and sanctify the holy purposes of these Your servants, N and N. By Your grace they have dedicated to You today this dwelling and all who live in it, to be a dwelling also for the Most Holy Trinity. Help them to serve You always in this little Church You have entrusted to their authority and love, to raise their children in the fear and love of Your Name, and to be a united witness, within Your Church Universal, to the new and eternal life won by Christ's redemption. Grant these prayers through Jesus Christ, Your Son, our Lord, Who lives and reigns with You in the unity of the Holy Spirit, One God, world without end.

R: Amen.

Solemn Blessing

Priest/Deacon: God our Father made you children by water and the Holy Spirit: may He bless you and watch over you with His fatherly love.

R: Amen.

Priest/Deacon: Jesus Christ, the Son of God, promised that the Spirit of truth would be with His Church forever; may He bless you and give you courage in professing the true faith.

R: Amen.

Priest/Deacon: The Holy Spirit came down upon the disciples and set their hearts on fire with love: may He bless you, keep you one in faith and love, and bring you to the joy of God's kingdom.

R: Amen.

Priest/Deacon: May almighty God bless you, the Father, and the Son, ✝ and the Holy Spirit.

R: Amen.

Originally from the booklet The Priesthood of the Laity in the Domestic Church *by H. Lyman Stebbins. Used with permission.*

Lyman Stebbins also emphasizes the need of each home to have a space in the dwelling — but somewhat set apart — as a place of family gathering for prayer. This could be a room or even just a corner in a room with a prayer altar that receives some special care and décor that matches the liturgical season. Hopefully, in as much as possible, it should also be a place of silence conducive to prayer.

acknowledgements

I want to thank my wife Regina for urging me over the course of a number of years to compile this book. Indeed, if she hadn't started listing the prayers I commonly pray and asking me to add to the list, God knows if it otherwise would have been written. It at least would have taken much longer to produce if our friend Deacon Jim Findley had not invited me to speak at his diocesan deacons' conference, since the preparation for that talk compelled me to put together an initial edition to hand out at the event. I quickly realized that a table of contents and other elements were missing. The wedding of my daughter Joan to Ben Cantu provided the occasion for a more organized and expanded edition that was rushed to print in time for their summer wedding. The wedding reception almost completely depleted that print run and we still had requests for more copies. So my wife and I made time to fill in what was lacking in the previous versions in order to produce a far more comprehensive edition which you are now holding. In all of these endeavors, I thank God for the mysterious workings of His Divine Providence.

www.ingramcontent.com/pod-product-compliance
Lightning Source LLC
Chambersburg PA
CBHW021543150726
47990CB00006B/2381